The First-Year Experience Monograph Series No. 7

Supplemental Instruction:

Improving First-Year Student Success in High-Risk Courses

3rd edition

Marion E. Stone and Glen Jacobs, Editors

$$0.675m = \frac{X}{0.275\cdot}$$

**National Resource Center for
The First-Year Experience®
& Students in Transition**
UNIVERSITY OF SOUTH CAROLINA

2008

Co-sponsor
International Center for SI
University of Missouri-Kansas City

Cite as:

Stone, M. E., & Jacobs, G. (Eds.). (2008). *Supplemental instruction: Improving first-year student success in high-risk courses* (Monograph No. 7, 3rd ed.). Columbia, SC: University of South Carolina, National Resource Center for The First-Year Experience and Students in Transition.

Sample chapter citation:

Hurley, M., & Gilbert, M. (2008). Basic supplemental instruction model. In M. E. Stone & G. Jacobs (Eds.), *Supplemental instruction: Improving first-year student success in high-risk courses* (Monograph No. 7, 3rd ed., pp. 1-9) Columbia, SC: University of South Carolina, National Resource Center for The First-Year Experience and Students in Transition.

ISBN 978-1-889271-62-0

The First-Year Experience® is a service mark of the University of South Carolina. A license may be granted upon written request to use the term "The First-Year Experience." This license is not transferable without written approval of the University of South Carolina.

Special thanks to Tracy L. Skipper, Editorial Projects Coordinator, for project management and editing; to Trish Willingham, Editor, and Dottie Weigel and Dana Fish, Graduate Assistants, for copyediting and proofing; and to Angie Mellor, Graphic Artist, for design and layout.

Additional copies of this monograph may be obtained from the National Resource Center for The First-Year Experience and Students in Transition, University of South Carolina, 1728 College Street, Columbia, SC 29208. Telephone (803) 777-6229. Fax (803) 777-4699.

Cataloging-in-Publication Data

Supplemental instruction : improving first-year student success in high-risk courses / Marion E. Stone and Glen Jacobs, editors. -- 3rd ed.

    p. cm. -- (First-year experience monograph series ; no. 7)

Includes bibliographical references.

ISBN 978-1-889271-62-0

1. College student development programs--United States. 2. College States. I. Stone, Marion E. II. Jacobs, Glen.

LB2343.4.S93 2008

378.1'98--dc22

                   2008014020

Contents

Foreword

Glen Jacobs and Marion E. Stone

It is a pleasure to present these writings on Supplemental Instruction (SI) as part of The First-Year Experience monograph series for the National Resource Center for The First-Year Experience and Students in Transition. In 1992, the University of Missouri – Kansas City's Center for Academic Development wrote a first edition of this monograph, *Supplemental Instruction: Improving First-Year Student Success in High-Risk Courses,* which focused on the development, implementation, and expansion of the program in its first two decades and examined how the program contributed to student learning. The first edition was reprinted with minor revisions a year later. We offer this new edition as an opportunity to explore the subsequent progression of SI and offer a practical resource for educators seeking to implement a new program or revamp an existing one.

SI came about as an alternative to traditional programs such as individual tutoring, study skills sessions, developmental classes, and the practice in higher education of targeting high-risk students, a population that is often difficult to define and challenging to support. The conventional means of classifying such students—standardized test scores, high school ranking/grade point average, aptitude screening results, student self-referral—had proven to be problematic estimators of students' success in higher education. Not only were such efforts often inaccurate, they were also time-consuming, expensive, and viewed negatively by students who link even the best-intended support efforts with remediation. Therefore, the founding principle of SI was to shift the focus away from high-risk students to high-risk courses, those that consistently generate a 30% or higher rate of Ds, Fs, and Ws (withdrawals). These courses are often large classes that provide students little opportunity for interaction with the professor or with other students; have infrequent examinations that focus on complex, cognitively challenging material; include large amounts of reading and information; and have voluntary and or unrecorded class attendance. Such courses are also traditionally taught by instructors who demand a great deal of higher-level critical thinking.

As John Gardner suggested in the foreword of the first edition, by focusing on high-risk courses instead of high-risk students, SI takes on the role of providing a model of academic support for *all students*—where it is particularly needed—as an intervention for difficult first-year courses. Thus, SI offers an efficient means of providing academic support and avoids the remedial stigma that some students might associate with traditional assistance programs. Students from all ability levels, including students who want to improve their grades from a B to an A, feel comfortable taking advantage of SI support.

Now in its fourth decade, SI is a cost-effective, proven, academic-support model that is practiced on five continents. The SI model offers regularly scheduled, out-of-class, peer-facilitated review sessions to all students enrolled in a targeted course. The sessions are informal small-group discussions that emphasize the development of organizational skills, questioning techniques, and test preparation strategies in an effort to engage students in critical thinking and promote both their short- and long-term academic success. SI sessions provide a dynamic, collaborative approach to learning that incorporates a deeper discussion of course content with the application of important learning strategies. The outcomes of this program encourage critical thinking and changes to the way that many students approach learning.

The chapters that follow look at the structure of SI and the critical role SI can play in setting the stage for deeper understanding of course content, and ultimately, for improved learning. The chapters also focus on an overview of the model; a further examination of SI that includes data outcomes; learning theories that underpin SI; various strategies for program implementation; recruitment, selection, and training of leaders; session strategies for various academic disciplines; expansion of SI to a video-based program; and international adaptations and future directions for the program. We hope you find this informative and helpful as you design and implement programs for first-year and other students in transition.

Thirty-Five Years of Supplemental Instruction: Reflections on Study Groups and Student Learning

F. Kim Wilcox and Glen Jacobs

For the past 35 years, The University of Missouri – Kansas City (UMKC) has provided training in Supplemental Instruction (SI) to more than 1,500 colleges and universities in 29 countries. Here, we attempt to identify some of the insights we have gained about teaching and learning from our own practice of providing academic support through facilitated study groups and from our relationships with the institutions with whom we have partnered in training. Part of the function of education is to make familiar things sound strange and strange things sound familiar. Much of what we have learned the reader will find both familiar and strange.

The Relationship Between Teaching and Talking

Asked about the best way for students to learn something, instructors may respond that it is to teach it to someone else. Our strategy for helping students master challenging course content has been guided by a concentrated effort to get participants thinking about and talking about difficult concepts. A perfect world, from the SI perspective, is to have students talking to students about difficult course content, as soon as possible, as much as possible, and for as long as possible. To talk is to teach and to teach is to learn. Whoever does most of the talking does most of the learning because talking requires prerequisite critical thinking. That is, the requirements placed on the brain when it is attempting to articulate issues surrounding a topic are different than the requirements placed on the brain when it is simply familiarizing itself with a topic. The first process is active; whereas, the second is passive. It is similar to the differences one might find in writing an article versus reading one. Writing requires a deeper level of engagement than reading, because generating a structure for information is a more involved process than trying to absorb it as it is being presented.

Furthermore, instructors cannot be certain that learning is taking place simply because the information is being delivered. Not until the instructor actually hears the learner talk about what he or she knows can the instructor assume that an understanding has developed. Believing that a message has been received just because it was delivered is the oral equivalent of an optical illusion. This illusion happens because the instructor, through the process of delivering the course material, is learning, and assumes the students are having a similar experience. They are not. Teaching the material represents the conclusion of a process of learning for the speaker, but it is only the introduction of the process for the listener. If the final goal of the learning process is assimilation, this can only be achieved as the learner engages the material at the level of articulating his or her understanding of it. Teaching and learning are problematic precisely because nothing in the experience of teaching warns instructors that students are not at the same stage of the learning process as the instructor. It is only when the roles are reversed, and the student is given the opportunity to act as the instructor, that the process of learning becomes complete.

The act of articulating what one understands about any given subject is the core activity of critical thinking. One can listen without thinking, but one cannot talk without thinking. This is not to say that all talking necessarily reflects sound thinking—only that it is impossible to talk without engaging a topic at a deeper level of involvement than is required by listening.

So, a central component of SI has been providing academic support to students taking historically difficult courses and to provide them with a structure where they could talk to and teach each other. But why the emphasis on students talking to each other? Would it not be better if they engaged the instructor in a dialogue? Perhaps, but the problem is that students typically will not talk if the instructor is present. The difficulty is not that instructors lack the will or ability to facilitate an in-class discussion; most instructors do allow time for and encourage class discussions. The problem is that course instructors are not the best candidates for leading a discussion because the power differential between students and instructors is difficult to overcome, especially for first-year students, and because of constraints inherent in the classroom setting.

Why Students Will Not Talk to Instructors

Saying that the instructor is an obstacle to authentic classroom discussion is, in no way, a reflection on the instructor's professional ability, personal communication competence, or level of awareness about the value of an interactive classroom. It is simply a comment on the inescapability of the instructor's position. The instructor is typically an expert on the course content and, ironically, this is the root of the problem. In the presence of experts, our tendency is to remain silent, to let them do the talking. Experts are experts because they already have everything figured out. Our natural and assumed role when we are in their presence is reduced to making sense of what they are saying—to listen and gather information. A more critical and less dependent involvement with the information may occur later when we are given the opportunity to add our voice to the discussion. When providing academic support, we have attempted to foster a structure for discussion by intentionally removing the instructor/expert from the discussion. When the instructor/expert is no longer present, students must become the experts and, consequently, may feel compelled to talk.

A great deal of what passes for in-class discussion is not discussion at all, but rather, an academic game of "guess what is in my head." The game is played when the instructor asks a series of questions with predetermined (at least from the students' perspective) answers and calls on students who know the answers to raise their hands to confirm that they do, indeed, know what is in the instructor's head. This game may be useful to the extent that it allows instructors to assess what students already know, but it is not the best tool for facilitating learning. Learning is not so much about what one already knows, but rather, what one is attempting to understand. The kind of discussion that best facilitates learning takes place when we are unsure of what we know and, by discussing it, attempt to sort it out. Students, who answer in-class questions, typically do so because they believe it is expedient to bring it to the instructor's attention that they do, indeed, *know* the answer. However, the students who could benefit most from attempting to answer questions are those who are least likely to do so because they are also the ones who are the least sure of their answers. During in-class discussions, students weigh their comments carefully and consider the potential effect any comment may have on their standing with the instructor. Students rarely lose sight of the fact that the instructor, however open and gracious he or she may be, is also the person who issues grades at the end of the term. Even if there is no correlation between students' in-class comments and their assigned grades, students still perceive that this may be the case. This dynamic necessarily dictates that there will be structural hurdles already in place when it comes to in-class discussion and exploring an issue purely for the sake of learning.

Another reason why students do not participate in class discussions is because there is not enough time. Simple rules of group dynamics suggest that the more people you have in a group, the less opportunity each group member has to contribute to the discussion. There simply is not enough time for the instructor to engage each student in a dialogue about the issues and check for understanding. To improve student learning, we must find ways to actively involve students in discussions. Time constraints dictate that some of these discussions must necessarily take place outside of class.

Preparing for Class Outside of Class

The key to improving student learning in college courses does not occur during class; it is what happens outside of class. The fastest gains to be made in student learning can most likely be made by improving the manner in which students prepare for class. Most students are given little or no training in how to master the art of homework. Preparation for class is typically reduced to the following formula: Students should study two hours outside of class for every hour in class. First of all, we have yet to meet the student who actually followed this formula, and secondly, it misses the point by not focusing on what students should be doing during those two hours. Through SI, we have learned a great deal about the need for structure in how students approach their homework.

Our study sessions are typically facilitated by a student who knows both the professor and the course for which we are organizing study sessions. The ideal facilitator focuses on more than the course content; he or she guides students through the process of how to think about and prepare for class sessions. SI leaders do more than facilitate review sessions; they actually coach students in good student behavior by modeling the kinds of behaviors that good students practice. It is these behaviors, not a formula for time, that eventually result in content mastery and good grades. Many students think that "A" students are naturally smart; they are unaware of the strategies these students employ to achieve good grades. Thus, it is important that less-successful students have an opportunity to witness firsthand how an "A" student prepares for class. The processes that lead to academic success should not be shrouded in mystery. Weaker students are sometimes lost, not because they lack the intellectual capabilities, but because they do not know where to begin. Their efforts seem lacking because their approach is wrong, and their approach is wrong because they do not have one. Good students, on the other hand, are good students, at least in part, because they have become adept at reading the expectations of the professor, predicting the direction of the course, and developing good study habits and ways of thinking about the course. Skilled facilitators do more than cover the course content; they demystify the process of how good students go about getting good grades.

Expectation That Something Should Make Sense

A familiar story in SI lore is of the student who misunderstood the professor's lecture on religious sects. In his or her notes, the student had written "religious sex" instead of "religious sects." When the SI leader pointed out that religious sex made no sense "at a whole bunch of different levels," one of the students reminded him that instructors often say things that do not make sense and that students write it down and try to memorize it anyway. In other words, students frequently have no expectation that the course material should make sense or fit together in a cohesive manner. Yet, it is difficult for students to learn when the act of learning is no longer clearly defined as something that should actually make sense. Students believe much of the content they are required to learn has little or no direct application to their lives or future plans. Hence, they invest as little energy as possible in understanding the material. Their plan will eventfully backfire, however, because most college-level courses require that students demonstrate more overall content understanding than mere memorization allows. For many students, this may be the first time in their schooling process that they have had to make this distinction. When they begin to approach the material with the idea that it should make sense, they have taken the first and most important step in the learning process.

Conclusion

At the core, our practice in SI has taught us much about how students learn. To summarize, (a) students learn best when they talk to each other; (b) talking to each other will be more effective if the instructor is not present for every discussion; (c) study sessions need to be organized outside of class; (d) to keep the sessions on task, you will probably need a trained facilitator who, preferably, knows both the course and the instructor; and (e) it is important for students to approach the course like it is *supposed* to make sense instead of just trying to memorize the right answer.

Thirty-five years is a long time in educational program years. We have seen a great number of ideas and programs come and go. Many of them were good ideas, and we have been happy to borrow from them and grateful for all they had to teach us. There is little that is new in the practice of education and the learning process, but there is still much we can learn about our students and how our practices can serve them better. We continue to learn as we go, and the everyday practice of Supplemental Instruction continues to amaze us with its strange and familiar qualities.

Chapter 1

Basic Supplemental Instruction Model

Maureen Hurley and Melinda Gilbert

Supplemental Instruction (SI) is a peer-led academic assistance program that targets traditionally difficult courses and is offered to all students enrolled in the supported classes. The peer-led sessions are held three or four times a week in an informal seminar during which students compare notes, discuss readings and concepts, clarify issues of confusion, and solve complex problems. The continual practice of these strategies within the session creates deeper engagement with and enhanced learning of the material. Students' critical thinking and reasoning skills are further developed through this small-group approach to learning (University of Missouri – Kansas City, 2004). Students begin to develop their own learning strategies through the guidance of an SI leader—a student who has already been successful in the class and was recommended by the course instructor.

SI began in 1973 at the University of Missouri – Kansas City (UMKC) as a way to decrease the attrition rate among students in the university's professional schools. Medical and dental school students were experiencing higher failure/withdrawal rates in science courses (e.g., anatomy and physiology) than would be expected, based on the caliber of the schools' admitted student body. Gary Widmar (1994), the vice-chancellor of student affairs, received a grant to address the specific retention problem and asked Deanna Martin, a doctoral student in education and instructor of a first-year study skills course, to identify a solution.

After examining the research on learning and retention and contacting academic support centers, Martin discovered that most learning centers were isolated from the mainstream of their campuses, offering ancillary services. Academic support providers were challenged to identify students who needed assistance because standardized tests were not particularly helpful in predicting who would experience academic difficulty. Remedial programs and courses were being added to already heavy student loads. Transferability of study skills was undocumented, and students often did not ask for help in a timely manner. Institutions did not support programs financially, and evaluations of the services were frequently missing.

Martin, as part of her research, visited the Student Learning Center at UC Berkeley, where Martha Maxwell was doing research on student learning, and came away with a key insight: Study skills instruction worked best when applied to specific course content. This insight became the impetus for the design and development of the Supplemental Instruction model, a program whose goal was to reduce attrition without lowering rigorous academic standards.

The program she envisioned had to be nonremedial, cost effective, able to be evaluated, and agreeable to faculty. As a result, she decided to focus on historically high-risk courses instead of high-risk students. Rather than placing blame on the students or the professor, SI provides additional academic support, enabling students to learn the necessary skills to master difficult course content. Arendale (1994) explained,

> The characteristics that identify a course as being historically difficult or 'high-risk' include: large amounts of weekly readings from both difficult textbooks and secondary library reference works, infrequent examinations that focus on high cognitive levels, voluntary and unrecorded class attendance, and large classes in which each student has little opportunity for interaction with the professor or the other students. (p. 11)

The results for the initial pilot at UMKC were immediately encouraging. In courses supported by SI, the percentages of the top grades rose, while the number of withdrawals fell. SI was not seen as remedial because it began the first week of class before any tests had been given, and all students were offered the opportunity to participate in the program. The program cost little to operate, and it required a minimum amount of faculty time. Martin soon discovered, and research later confirmed, that the students who participated in SI sessions scored higher on test grades and a smaller percentage of them failed or withdrew from the class than non-SI participants (Blanc, DeBuhr, & Martin, 1983; Martin, 1980; Martin & Blanc, 1981). The success of the pilot ensured SI's place at UMKC.

After the initial pilot in the early 1970s, SI was implemented in UMKC's Schools of Dentistry, Medicine, and Pharmacy. At that time, its potential as a campus-wide program became apparent. It soon expanded to the UMKC College of Arts and Sciences and has grown into a national and international program. Individuals from more than 1,500 higher education institutions in 29 countries have been trained in the SI model. SI was recognized by the U.S. Department of Education as an Exemplary Educational Practice in 1981. The model is still beneficial to students, as they continue to earn high grades, and provides valuable feedback to faculty. In some institutions, SI has been adopted as a model to promote more student-centered teaching. The program also supports cultural diversity, critical thinking, rigorous academic standards, and retention.

Selection of Courses

First-year courses are usually selected for SI, especially those with a 30% or higher rate of D, F, and withdrawal (DFW) grades. Depending on the individual needs of an institution, the program may also target gatekeeper and prerequisite courses required for certain majors. Class size is another consideration. Large classes make it difficult for SI sessions to maintain the small-group format, and small classes make it hard to keep attendance sufficient for effective SI sessions. Once these criteria have been considered, a decision must be made regarding who among the faculty will be most receptive to having SI attached to their courses (University of Missouri – Kansas City, 2004)

Student Characteristics

Even students who did well in high school may experience some academic challenges when making the transition to college. Some students may enter the university underprepared and with little exposure to the rigors of college courses. Others may find it difficult to listen to a lecture and take a useful and meaningful set of notes. Still other students may have trouble selecting main ideas from lectures, reading lengthy chapters in textbooks, and making sense of key concepts and themes. These struggles may impact students' motivation to learn, which is critical to academic success (Tinto, 1993). Closely tied to motivation are feelings of self-esteem and self-efficacy. When students feel ill-equipped for the challenges of college, their self-worth and confidence are deeply affected (Tinto).

SI literature often refers to the dependency cycle or learned helplessness, a pattern that results in students becoming dependent upon an authority figure for answers. In a university setting, this authority figure is the instructor or tutor, who might provide information in a repetitious manner. Many students can memorize information in this setting, but not truly learn. When students have questions or do not understand certain concepts, the professor or tutor often merely repeats what he or she already stated. Sometimes, the information is even provided at a slower pace, in the hope that the students will understand. Eventually, the professor or tutor may give up trying to explain the idea or concept and will move on to the next topic, without the student ever truly understanding the first concept. The next time students have questions, the cycle starts all over again. After a while, students may feel like they just cannot learn or understand complicated information and might give up. SI strives to break this cycle by encouraging students to find their own answers to questions instead of depending on the professor or tutor.

In particular, SI helps students overcome the dependency cycle by offering them the opportunity to work in small groups on a regular basis. Research shows that students often learn more and feel more comfortable working in small groups and in nontraditional classroom arrangements (Goodsell, Maher, Tinto, Smith, & MacGregor, 1992). The camaraderie and synergy of the group can provide a social network, along with the realization that they are not the only ones trying to master difficult course material. This experience can improve self-image and allow students to view themselves as capable of mastering concepts that eluded them in the lecture.

Vygotsky's (1978) theory of proximal development suggests that the synergy of a group is powerful and that what students learn collectively in a collaborative setting today can result in them becoming effective independent learners tomorrow. In SI, students become less and less dependent on one another and on the leader, increasingly relying on their own abilities. Students also become less reliant on being told information. This approach to learning can certainly benefit students at all skill levels; thus, it does not carry a remedial image.

The establishment of rapport that occurs in the SI session goes a long way toward providing both an academic and social support mechanism for students. Since many students make their decision to remain at or leave an institution in the first few weeks (Tinto, 1993), it is important to provide interventions, such as SI, that keep students from feeling disconnected from the college or university. Students who do not forge a meaningful connection to a faculty member or peer may leave the institution. Therefore, it is critical that students have experiences that engage and empower them and place them at the center of the learning process.

Metacognition, evaluating strategies for learning and identifying which strategies work well for certain types of assignments and exams, is invaluable to students who may not have a clue as to the best way to study. Many students have never thought about the processes involved in learning. They need to be guided in this direction to become fully developed independent thinkers and learners (Tinto, 1993). SI can be instrumental in providing this guidance and in supporting the success of new students.

Although many educators might think of at-risk students as those who need the most help, high-achieving students are equally challenged in many instances. Wratcher (1991) conducted a study at Carnegie Mellon University that looked at students who had excelled academically in high school but who experienced some failure upon entering higher education. When these high-achieving students received a low test score or were challenged academically, they entered a state of denial. They often failed to seek help as they had never experienced the need before. They did not want to admit they could not meet the academic challenges alone. The denial was further complicated by stress (Martin & Arendale, 1993). SI can be an effective intervention for these previously high-achieving students by providing guided study opportunities that allow them to work in small groups and address their academic challenges.

Many selective institutions have found SI to be a good fit for their students, particularly those who wish to major in the hard sciences. These students may become discouraged or barred from a desired major by failing to make a high enough grade in a prerequisite course. The Consortium on High Achievement and Success (CHAS) is composed of more than 35 small, private, liberal arts colleges and universities with students who are among the brightest and best prepared in the nation upon entering college. Yet, many of those students fail to achieve their highest potential. Over the last several years, a number of CHAS schools have implemented SI as part of their programming to address this issue. Reports from members of CHAS have shown students are achieving higher mean final course grades and fewer DFW grades than comparable students in previous years.

Essential Individuals

SI Leaders

The SI leader is a student who has previously taken the target course, is deemed content competent, is recommended and approved by the professor, and has been trained in proactive learning and study strategies. Martin chose to use peers as SI leaders because she found that students feel more comfortable learning with peers. Students can ask peers questions and not worry about "looking stupid" or having their lack of understanding impact their grade. The SI leader guides students in learning appropriate applications of study strategies such as note taking, graphic organizers (visual learning aids such as concept maps or matrices), questioning techniques, vocabulary acquisition, and test preparation. However, the leader's facilitation skills are equally important. The SI sessions are meant to be opportunities for students to grapple with difficult concepts and solve complex problems. Unless the leader can plan effective sessions that allow students to teach one another, SI becomes merely an add-on to the lecture. The SI leader must also structure the session in such a way that all students have the opportunity to participate and demonstrate what they have learned. If needed, the leader can step in to keep students on track.

SI Supervisor

The supervisor/program coordinator is a full-time, professional staff member with a number of responsibilities. This individual must plan the program, interview and select leaders, set up and conduct initial and ongoing training sessions, help plan and observe sessions, and establish and maintain strong relationships with the faculty. In addition to daily management of the program, the SI supervisor is charged with program evaluation and expansion. All academic programs encounter unexpected problems, so the supervisor also needs to be a problem solver and a troubleshooter.

Faculty Members

Faculty members associated with target courses play a key role in the success of SI. It is advantageous if faculty are interested in and enthusiastic about the SI program. For example, faculty should allow SI leaders to attend lectures, be available to meet with the leaders during office hours to approve their SI session plans, and provide feedback, as needed.

Students

Students are the key individuals served by the SI program. Students are encouraged to attend as many SI sessions as they feel they need, but SI sessions are usually voluntary.

SI Leader Training

Once SI leaders have been selected for the target classes, new and returning SI leaders attend a one-to two-day, preterm training workshop, as well as regularly scheduled training meetings throughout the semester. The fundamentals of the SI model are addressed in the preterm training workshop. SI leaders also have the opportunity to practice important SI strategies, observe established SI leaders, participate in team-building exercises, and simulate their own SI sessions. Because it is hard to be fully proficient in these skills after only two days of training, ongoing training with SI supervisors is important. SI leaders' skills are observed by an SI supervisor while on the job throughout the semester, so that any challenges can be addressed immediately.

SI Sessions

The group study sessions start during the first week of class and run throughout the semester, and the SI leader attends each class in order to model good student behavior such as note-taking. This also provides the leader with the opportunity to observe what concepts are particularly difficult for students to comprehend. The leader is then better prepared to structure the SI sessions around those elements. In the SI sessions, the leader facilitates discussion of key concepts, helping students to connect new information to past knowledge. The SI leader is trained in collaborative learning strategies and uses small-group strategies to enhance learning and study skills (rather than a lecture). The sessions provide students with additional time to think critically and engage with the content. Thinking aloud and questioning one another helps students develop articulation skills in a comfortable environment. During the semester, the sessions not only provide opportunities to process information but also to review and prepare for exams. Students learn to predict exam questions and practice answering them in the format in which the test is given.

Learning Strategies in SI

Students may be used to memorizing and retaining all kinds of information for a short time and may have even done reasonably well using this strategy in high school. They quickly discover in college that they cannot rely too much on drill and memorization; rather, they must develop new and more effective techniques. Many students do not have a toolbox of learning strategies that allows them to understand, retain, and retrieve important and meaningful information that they can generalize across subjects. The key to using effective learning strategies in SI sessions is to integrate them into the course content rather than to think of them as individual "study skills." By modeling and demonstrating appropriate strategies, leaders can assist students in developing the kind of thinking and problem-solving skills that will help them master difficult course content.

Note-Taking

As a first step in helping students learn to take effective notes, the SI leader can look at the note-taking strategies being used. The leader can demonstrate effective ways that he or she has taken notes and point out students who are using sound techniques. Many students do not know how to listen to a lecture and summarize the important points. First-year students are encouraged to take notes as much as they can, bring their notes to SI sessions, and then, together with other students, the leader can guide them in formulating a good set of notes. Note-taking strategies should be addressed early in the semester before students become discouraged and lost in the lectures.

Learning to Work in Small Study Groups

Although students may initially be reticent about working in small study groups, they often find it beneficial, as they can rely on others to help them find the best way to organize large amounts of material and to study more effectively. The support of others is an added bonus for new students as they struggle to adjust to campus life. Students also find that thinking, talking out loud as they formulate their thoughts, and grappling with ideas from other students actually contribute to their understanding of the content.

Checking for Understanding

Checking for understanding is critical for the leader to find out what students understand about the most difficult and important concepts from the lectures. It is essential that the leader asks open-ended questions so that students can demonstrate their knowledge. They need to explain the steps in a problem or discuss a topic to show that they understand. Other ways to check for understanding include observing students for confusion, asking students to summarize a topic, asking for a volunteer to outline a topic, or asking a student to solve a similar problem and enumerate the steps that lead to a solution.

Redirecting Questions

Redirecting questions is a key process in SI and is based on the idea that we learn more effectively if we have to explain something to someone else. The goal is to encourage student interaction during the sessions. Thus, the SI leader uses redirecting statements to encourage students to talk to one another, rather than addressing all their questions to the leader. Examples of these include:

Student to leader: Who came up with the law of relativity?
Leader: Does someone have the answer to this question?

Student to leader: I don't know how to do this problem.
Leader: What part(s) of the problem do you understand?

Wait Time

There are two types of wait time: (a) the time that elapses after the leader has asked a question and (b) the time the leader takes after a response is made by a student. After the 5 to10 seconds of wait time, the leader can directly ask someone else, rephrase the question, give part of the answer, or ask students what part of the question they can answer. The leader should also wait several seconds before saying anything or calling on someone else, as students need time to think critically and formulate well-thought-out responses. Research shows that students' understanding and level of response improves with longer wait time.

Exam Preparation and Debriefing

The SI sessions in the final week before an exam can focus on students' polishing the skills that they have learned. A good, well-planned review can help lessen students' anxiety regarding an upcoming test. The leader can also offer test-taking tips, such as strategies for identifying which questions to answer first and reading and outlining test questions carefully. After each exam, the leader conducts a post-exam review with students. This process can help students figure out what worked well and in what areas they were deficient in preparing for the exam. The first exam gives students a definite idea of the kinds of questions the professor asks, which can help them identify what they need to focus on for future exams.

SI Outcomes

Regardless of ethnicity and prior academic achievement, students who participate in SI sessions (a) earn higher average final course grades, (b) have lower DFW rates, (c) re-enroll at higher rates, and (d) have higher graduation rates than students who do not attend SI sessions. These outcomes are supported by numerous studies (Arendale & Martin, 1997; Bidgood, 1994; Blanc et al., 1983; Bushway & Flower, 2002; Congos & Schoeps, 2003; Martin, 1980; Martin & Arendale, 1993; Martin & Blanc, 1981; Martin, Blanc, & Arendale, 1996).

The students who attend SI sessions are not the only individuals who benefit from SI. The SI leaders benefit in a variety of areas, including improved academic abilities, new and better communication skills, professional interactions with faculty and administrators, greater self-confidence as their knowledge deepens, increased multicultural competency, and enhanced leadership skills (Stout & McDaniel, 2006). Faculty also benefit from having SI as a part of their courses. Theoretically, they can spend less time holding office hours for students who have difficulty with the course material because of the added resource of the SI leader, and they have more time for class preparation, research, and meetings. SI has also been used specifically as a faculty development tool, both formally and informally (Marshall, 1994; Zerger, Clark-Unite, & Smith, 2006).

Program Evaluation and Reporting

The purpose of evaluating the SI program is twofold: (a) to determine the effectiveness of the SI program and (b) to provide a rationale for institutional financial support. An evaluation should be completed at midterm and after final exams when final grades have been reported. In the evaluation, two items are measured: learning and retention. Learning is measured by the difference in mean final course grades. The SI group should score higher than the non-SI group, and the more often students participate in SI, the higher the mean final course grade should be. Retention is measured by DFW rates of a course. High DFW rates represent unsuccessful enrollments in a course. The assumption is that these high rates lead to eventual attrition from the institution. The DFW rates for the SI group should be significantly lower than that of the non-SI group.

End-of-term SI surveys are also handed out to students in classes supported by SI. This gives the students the opportunity to evaluate the SI leader's performance and give feedback on the perceived benefits of their SI experience. The survey also asks questions for those who did not attend SI sessions to find out their reasons for not attending, which helps the program consider changes to make SI available to as many students as possible.

Faculty and administrators will want to know how many students were served by the program and whether or not they benefited. The attendance data, end-of-term SI surveys, and the reports on mean final course grades and percentage rates of DFW grades should be sent along with a narrative report on each class to the appropriate faculty, chairs, deans, and administrators.

Lessons Learned

We have learned many lessons in our 35 years of experience running a successful SI program. First, we have found that SI does not work well when sessions are supporting an easy course, nor does it work well with a course that students perceive as easy, even if it is difficult. When a course is easy, or is perceived as easy, students do not have the motivation to attend SI sessions because they think they will receive their desired grade without the help of SI. Second, we have found that SI does not work well in a course with an instructor who does not support the program. The more an instructor supports SI, the more the instructor will promote its use. If the instructor does not feel as though SI will benefit his or her class, then neither will the students. Finally, SI does not work well when supporting more than one section of a course with only one leader. SI leaders are unable to attend multiple lectures, and the SI model does not work well when SI leaders do not attend class. SI leaders must attend lectures in order to have up-to-date information about course content and to be a role model for other students. Finally, being seen conversing with the instructor may lend credibility to the SI leader.

Conclusion

In a cost-effective manner, SI provides ongoing opportunities for students to effectively equip themselves with the necessary strategies to be successful academically from the outset of their college careers. SI is not only a sound strategy for working with small groups of students, but it is also an educational model with global implications. SI continues to expand internationally and in the United States, as more institutions are looking for models that help students succeed. According to Martin in her opening address at the International SI Conference in Boston in 2004, "There is no less need for SI than when we started. In fact, there is a great deal more." As long as institutions continue to enroll students with myriad academic support needs, there will be a place for SI.

References

Arendale, D. (1994). Understanding the Supplemental Instruction model. In D. C. Martin, & D. Arendale (Eds.), *Supplemental Instruction: Increasing achievement and retention* (pp. 11-22). San Francisco: Jossey-Bass.

Arendale, D., & Martin, D. C. (1997). *Review of research concerning the effectiveness of Supplemental Instruction from the University of Missouri – Kansas City and other Institutions.* Kansas City, MO: The University of Missouri – Kansas City.

Bidgood, P. (1994). The success of Supplemental Instruction: Statistical evidence. In C. Rust & J. Wallace (Eds.), *Helping students to learn from each other: Supplemental Instruction* (pp. 71-79). Birmingham, England: Staff and Educational Development Association.

Blanc, R. A., DeBuhr, L. E., & Martin, D. C. (1983). Breaking the attrition cycle: The effects of Supplemental Instruction on undergraduate performance and attrition. *Journal of Higher Education, 54,* 81-89.

Bushway, S. D., & Flower, S. M. (2002). Helping criminal justice students learn statistics: A quasi-experimental evaluation of learning assistance. *Journal of Criminal Justice Education, 13*(1), 36-56.

Congos, D. H., & Schoeps, N. (2003). Inside Supplemental Instruction sessions: One model of what happens that improve grades and retention revisited. *Journal of Student Centered Learning, 1*(3), 161-172.

Goodsell, A., Maher, M., Tinto, V., Smith, B. L., & MacGregor, J. (1992). *Collaborative learning: A sourcebook for higher education.* Washington, DC: National Center for Teaching, Learning, and Assessment (NCTLA).

Marshall, S. (1994). Faculty development through Supplemental Instruction. In D. C. Martin , & D. Arendale (Eds.), *Supplemental Instruction: Increasing achievement and retention.* (New Directions for Teaching and Learning No. 60, pp. 31-40). San Francisco: Jossey-Bass.

Martin, D. C. (1980). Learning centers in professional schools. In K. V. Lauridsen (Ed.), *Examining the scope of learning centers* (pp. 69-79). San Francisco: Jossey-Bass.

Martin, D. C. (2004, June). *Supplemental Instruction (SI): Past, present, and future.* A welcome address delivered at the 3rd International SI Conference, Boston, MA.

Martin, D. C., & Arendale, D. (1993). *Supplemental instruction: Improving first-year student success in high-risk courses* (Monograph No. 7, 2nd ed.). Columbia, SC: University of South Carolina, The National Resource Center for The Freshman Year Experience.

Martin, D. C., & Blanc, R. A. (1981). The learning center's role in retention: Integrating student support services with departmental instruction. *Journal of Developmental and Remedial Education, 4*(3), 2-4, 21-23.

Martin, D .C., Blanc, R. A., & Arendale, D. (1996). Supplemental Instruction: Supporting the classroom experience. In J. N. Hankin (Ed.), *The community college: Opportunity and access for America's first-year students* (Monograph No. 19, pp. 123-133). Columbia, SC: University of South Carolina, National Resource Center for The Freshman Year Experience and Students in Transition.

Stout, M. L., & McDaniel, A. (2006). Benefits to SI leaders. In M. E. Stone & G. Jacobs (Eds.), *Supplemental Instruction: New Visions for Empowering Student Learning.* (New Directions for Teaching and Learning No. 106, pp. 55-62). San Francisco: Jossey-Bass.

Tinto, V. (1993). *Leaving college: Rethinking the causes and cures of student attrition* (2nd ed.). Chicago: The University of Chicago Press.

University of Missouri – Kansas City. (2004). *Supplemental Instruction leader resource manual.* Kansas City, MO: The Curators of the University of Missouri.

Vygotsky, L. S. (1978). *Mind in society.* Cambridge, MA: Harvard University Press.

Widmar, G. E. (1994). Supplemental Instruction: From small beginnings to a national program. In D. C. Martin & D. Arendale (Eds.), *Supplemental Instruction: Increasing achievement and retention* (pp. 3-10). San Francisco: Jossey-Bass.

Wratcher, M. A. (1991). Freshman academic adjustment at a competitive university. *The College Student, 25*(2), 170-177.

Zerger, S., Clark-Unite, C., & Smith, L. (2006). How Supplemental Instruction benefits faculty, administration, and institutions. In M. E. Stone & G. Jacobs (Eds.), *Supplemental Instruction: New visions for empowering student learning.* (New Directions for Teaching and Learning No. 106, pp. 63-72). San Francisco: Jossey-Bass.

Chapter 2

Research on the Effectiveness of Supplemental Instruction

Maureen Hurley and Melinda Gilbert

Studies indicate that more than half of students entering colleges and universities for the first time will leave their initial institution before graduating (Tinto, 1993). As a result, schools have implemented academic support programs in order to reduce attrition. One program that has been shown to be effective in increasing retention and graduation rates for those who participate is Supplemental Instruction (SI) (Arendale & Martin, 1997; Blanc, DeBuhr, & Martin, 1983; Martin & Arendale, 1993a). SI, a peer-led, small-group study model, was developed to help students at all academic levels succeed in historically difficult courses. Moreover, the program design provides students with social opportunities to connect with fellow students and with their institution—an important factor that may contribute to student retention. This chapter reviews the research on the effectiveness of SI, highlighting its impact on retention and on other short- and long-term outcomes. For example, SI not only helps students achieve better scores in their current courses, but more important, it helps them master learning strategies that can be applied to additional coursework. Students, however, are not the only individuals who benefit from participating in SI sessions. SI leaders, usually students who have already taken the course and have been recommended by their professor, benefit through the acquisition of leadership skills gained from facilitating SI sessions.

Key Concepts of Student-Focused Learning

Underprepared students are arriving at colleges in record numbers; however, many institutions are still applying what Grubb (1998) calls a "standards-centered approach," focusing only on the basic material prescribed in the institutional standards for academic excellence that leaves these underprepared students at risk of dropping out within their first year. On the other hand, institutions whose missions focus on the needs of students more frequently adopt a constructivist pedagogy (i.e., the idea that learners construct knowledge for themselves) (Dewey, 1916; Kuh, Schuh, Witt, & Associates, 1991). These institutions implement active-learning models that take into account the interests and abilities of their students. Once these determinations are established, these institutions integrate a variety of educational

approaches into their curricular planning rather than relying only on traditional, instruction-based pedagogy. This section highlights some of the key concepts and related research that inform the SI model.
Because SI incorporates these components, it is expected that SI demonstrates similar outcomes to the
ones described here. Outcomes specific to SI will be examined in the remainder of the chapter. A more
detailed description of the theoretical frameworks influencing the SI model is included in chapter 3.

Collaborative Learning

How much information students retain from the lecture material is often debated. According to
Bok (2006), students retain 42% of a lecture by its end, 20% a week later, and considerably less over
time. Some research suggests that students retain much more of what they learn if they engage more
deeply with the material. Collaborative learning is one method of facilitating greater retention of and
engagement with course material.

Collaborative learning relies on peer interaction, creating a bridge between the instructor and the
students and, thus, removing a possible deterrent to learning. While meaningful learning seldom takes
place through the one-way transmission of knowledge (i.e., the lecture), teaching one another, which is
an interactive process, helps students construct and reinforce their own knowledge. Collaborative learning allows them to freely present their own ideas and comfortably disagree. Learning is not transferred
from instructor to student; rather knowledge is achieved through an interactive process. Students are
empowered to learn for themselves. Collaboration places knowledge with the community of participants,
rather than solely within the individual.

A proponent of cooperative learning and echoing a recommendation from Slavin (1990), Bok (2006)
suggests that each student should be accountable to the others and should make a contribution to the
learning process. Small group, collaborative learning creates a dynamic in which students rely on each
other, express ideas, and debate views—which sometimes leads to cognitive dissonance. This leads to
the development of new or alternative solutions and conclusions to problems.

Critical Thinking

Faculty agree that learning how to think critically is essential for students and is the principal goal
of undergraduate education (Bok, 2006). Because there is no universal set of analytical skills appropriate
for thinking about different kinds of problems, one must be able to adapt concepts to new situations.
Pascarella and Terenzini (1991; 2005) state that compared to first-year students, seniors are better at
abstract reasoning and critical thinking. They have greater intellectual flexibility and are better able to
understand more than one side of complex issues. Yet, Astin (1998) notes that two thirds of students
reported that they had not substantially improved their analytical skills from their first to their last year of
college. Bok suggests that faculty frequently do little to help students apply knowledge to new problems
and that there is a need to create a process of active learning by posing problems with challenging answers
and encouraging students to apply concepts to new situations. This is where Supplemental Instruction
becomes relevant. SI strategies are designed to help students learn how to think critically and pursue
answers to questions by themselves, or with peers, instead of relying on the instructor.

Outcomes Related to Supplemental Instruction

Academic Outcomes

Many studies have found that SI is effective in reducing attrition rates and increasing persistence
toward graduation (Arendale & Martin, 1997; Blanc et al., 1983; Martin & Arendale, 1993a; Martin

& Blanc, 1981; Martin, Blanc, & Arendale, 1996). Moreover, students who participate in SI are less likely to earn grades of D, F, or withdrawal (DFW) in a course (Arendale & Martin, 1994; Blanc et al.; Martin & Blanc; Martin & Arendale, 1993a; Martin et al., 1996). Research has also shown that the mean final course grades and grade point averages (GPAs) for students who attend SI are significantly higher than for those who do not attend (Arendale, 1996; Arendale & Martin; Blanc & Martin, 1994; Martin & Arendale, 1993a). For example, Blanc et al. (1983) conducted a study that compared a sample of high-risk students (those who scored below the 25th percentile on university admissions tests) who attended SI sessions with a similar sample of students who did not attend sessions. They found that students who participated in SI sessions showed significant gains in course grades compared to those who did not ($p < .01$). They also found that those who attended SI had significantly lower DFW rates than those who did not attend SI sessions ($p < .05$).

SI has also been used to assist conditionally admitted students in their transition to college. These students are frequently ill-prepared academically, socially, and/or organizationally (Ogden, Thompson, Russell, & Simons, 2003). Hodges (2001) compared the GPAs of 103 students who were conditionally admitted to a large state university in the southern United States who attended SI sessions with students who did not. He found that the SI participants earned significantly higher GPAs than non-SI participants ($p < .05$).

A comprehensive study conducted by the International Center for SI at the University of Missouri – Kansas City examined data from 37 institutions over three years (2003-2006) to determine if students who participated in SI earned higher course grades and withdrew from courses at lower rates. The average GPA for those who attended SI for all courses combined was 2.63 compared with 2.18 for those who did not attend (Figure 1). Of those who attended SI sessions in all two- and four-year colleges combined, 18.07% received a DFW grade, while those who did not attend SI had a 30.61% DFW rate (Figure 2).

Bidgood (1994) collected and analyzed data to determine the success of SI at Kingston University, UK, in a wide range of courses and degree programs, including computer science, electronics with computing and business, higher national diploma in electronic engineering, information systems design, chemistry, mathematics, estate management, civil engineering, biomedical science, and history. The results showed that despite similar entry qualifications and pre-SI attendance performance, the students who attended SI did significantly better in their courses than those who did not attend SI ($p < .05$).

Hensen and Shelley (2003) discovered that SI participants in biology, chemistry, mathematics, and physics courses at a large, public midwestern university earned a significantly higher percentage of A and B grades, a lower percentage of DFWs, and higher mean final course grades than non-SI participants in those classes. Adjustments for ACT score differences between groups did not change the results that SI participants had higher final course grades on average ($p < .05$).

A study performed by Jones and Fields (2001) showed a positive relationship between SI participation and academic performance in a Principles of Accounting class where students attended SI sessions on either a voluntary or mandatory basis. Significant performance differences were found between the voluntary attendees and mandatory attendees; however, the SI attendees outperformed the non-SI attendees even after controlling for students' SAT scores and prior academic performance ($p < .001$).

Congos and Schoeps (2003) used a chi-square test to compare SI and non-SI attendees' final course grades in a biology class and found that SI attendees made a significantly higher percentage of A, B, and C grades and a significantly lower percentage of D, F, and W grades than the non-SI attendees ($p < .01$). To control for differences between the groups, Congos and Schoeps analyzed SAT scores and school class rank. They found that SI students had SAT scores and predicted GPAs that were not significantly different from those of non-SI students (ancova, $p < .01$).

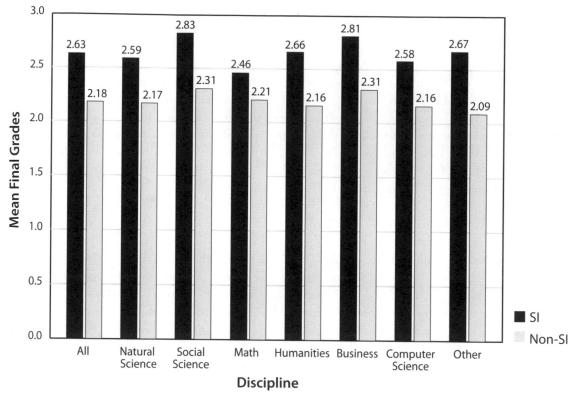

Figure 1. Mean grades for SI and non-SI participants by academic discipline. Data were collected from 1,003 courses at 37 institutions, with a total enrollment of 119,009 students. All differences are statistically significant at the .01 level except computer science, which is statistically significant a the .05 level.

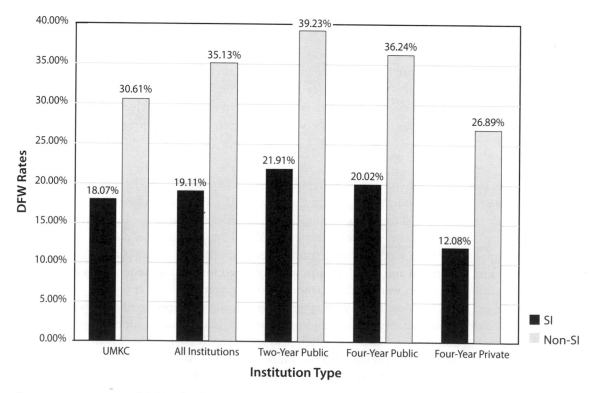

Figure 2. Percentage of DFW final course grades for SI and non-SI participants separated by institution type. Data were collected from 1,003 courses at 37 institutions, with a total enrollment of 119,009 students. All differences are statistically significant at the .001 level.

Affective Development

Another important aspect of a student's success is affective development, including self-efficacy. If a student feels like he or she cannot succeed because of the difficulty of course content, then most likely he or she will not succeed. Despite the importance of self-efficacy to academic success, few studies regarding the impact of SI on affective development have been undertaken. Visor, Johnson, and Cole (1992) performed one of the first studies to address the relationship of SI to affective development. They wanted to answer the following questions: Are students who participate in SI sessions more likely to have an internal locus of control (i.e., the feeling of being in charge of one's destiny), and will participation in SI reinforce that orientation? Will students with stronger feelings of self-efficacy be more apt to participate in SI, and will the experience of doing so make them feel more efficacious? Will students with lower self-esteem (i.e., beliefs about one's ability to succeed at a given task) be more likely to choose to participate in SI and will SI increase their self-esteem? Differences in self-efficacy were found between regular SI participants and occasional and nonparticipants ($p < .055$), though these were not statistically significant. A pairwise comparison follow-up test was performed and showed a significant difference between the regular participants and the occasional participants when it came to locus of control ($p < .05$). Regular participants had a significantly higher level of internal locus of control than the occasional participants. The difference between the regular participants and nonparticipants approached significance as well ($p < .1$). The occasional participants had the lowest self-esteem, and the follow-up tests revealed the same results ($p < .05$). Visor et al. (1992) indicated that even though little can be concluded from the lack of significance, all groups moved toward greater internal locus of control.

Visor, Johnson, Schollaet, Good-Majah, and Davenport (1995) performed a follow-up study to the Visor et al. (1992) study. They wanted to determine whether positive change in affective variables was related to participation in SI. The affective variables they studied included locus of control and self-esteem. To measure these variables, they used the Internal-External Control Scale (Rotter, 1976), the Self-Efficacy Scale (Sherer et al., 1987), and the Index of Self-esteem (Hudson, 1987).

Visor et al. (1995) found that first-year students who regularly participated in SI sessions tended to have (a) higher self-esteem, (b) greater self-efficacy, and (c) greater internal locus of control than first-year students who did not participate or who only occasionally participated, though differences in locus of control were not significant. Upper-level students who regularly attended SI sessions experienced similar outcomes, although the differences in self-efficacy for participants and nonparticipants or occasional participants was not statistically significant. Data are very limited in this area. More controlled studies need to be conducted to assess the relationship between SI and affective development.

Long-Term Gains

Research has indicated that students who regularly participate in SI experience long-term gains (Gattis, 2000; Martin, 1980; Ogden et al., 2003; Ramirez, 1997). For example, Ramirez conducted a longitudinal study of fall 1991 SI and non-SI participants in order to answer the following questions: What benefits are gained by students academically beyond the SI-supported target course (a course chosen because of high DFW rates)? Does SI participation strengthen the persistence patterns of particular student populations? Traditional and at-risk groups were followed for eight semesters from fall 1991 to spring 1995. Traditional students were students whose academic preparation at entry met all university requirements. At-risk students were those who where academically underprepared when entering the university or who had special academic needs and/or socioeconomic or education disadvantages. Traditional students who attended SI sessions regularly had significantly higher target course grades and GPAs compared to traditional students who did not attend ($p < .001$). At-risk students who attended SI sessions made significantly greater gains in target course grades and GPAs compared to at-risk students who did not attend SI sessions ($p < .001$). Ramirez concluded that the immediate impact of SI was statistically significant.

The long-term benefits of SI were best understood by comparing how these student groups performed before fall 1991 with their performance in spring 1995. SI allowed students to maintain the academic record they had established previously despite the added difficulty of a high-risk course. Traditional students who participated in SI improved the GPA they had prior to fall 1991 ($p < .0001$); however, nonparticipating traditional students performed poorly in the target course. As a result, their GPA's were significantly lower when that course was included in the calculation of their GPA. The high-risk students who did not attend SI dropped into the probation zone in the target course and moved much closer to the probation zone in their semester GPA. The at-risk students who attended SI sessions had significantly higher four-year retention rates (70%) compared to at-risk students who did not attend SI sessions (51%, $p < .01$). These findings were very encouraging because the at-risk students began college less prepared than the traditional students, but they were able to develop the skills they were lacking upon college entry (Ramirez, 1997).

Ogden et al. (2003) and Gattis (2000) also performed studies on the short- and long-term impact of SI. Ogden et al. found that conditionally admitted students participating in SI had significantly better short- and long-term outcomes compared to conditional non-SI participants. Conditional SI participants had higher target course grades ($p < .05$), fall 1995 GPA ($p < .01$), and cumulative GPA ($p < .01$) than the conditional non-SI participants or non-SI participants who were traditional admits. Conditional SI participants also reenrolled at higher rates; 88.3% enrolled by spring 1997 compared to 65.2% of conditional nonparticipants. Ogden et al. argued that because conditional SI participants had higher fall quarter GPAs compared to the conditional non-SI group, participants may have applied the skills and learning strategies practiced in SI sessions to other courses taken during the SI quarter.

Gattis (2000) explored short- and long-term grade improvements for chemistry students participating in SI at a large southwestern university. In the study, Gattis tracked SI attendance data, student performance predictors, and grade results. The participants included students who attended SI sessions in Chemistry I during the fall semester 1997 and in Chemistry II during the spring 1998 semester as well as students who attended SI sessions in Chemistry I during the fall semester and in Organic I during the spring semester. The study showed a relationship between spring SI attendance and higher Chemistry II grades and a relationship between fall 1997 Chemistry I SI attendance and higher spring 1998 Organic I grades. Students who attended SI during both fall and spring semesters had the highest average spring course grades ($p < .05$). Gattis concluded that the strong relationship between fall 1997 Chemistry I SI attendance and spring 1998 Organic Chemistry grades would seem to make the case for long-term learning effects. However, Gattis acknowledges that other factors may have an impact on students' improvement in grades, such as motivation, work ethic, and self-esteem, and that these factors could have been present prior to SI attendance. More studies need to be performed with these factors taken into consideration to determine the long-term impact of Supplemental Instruction.

Impact on SI Leaders

While participants benefit greatly from attending SI sessions on a regular basis, SI leaders also benefit from being a part of the program. However, the empirical research exploring outcomes for SI leaders is limited. Stout and McDaniel (2006) performed a qualitative research study on the impact of SI on its leaders. They reported that some of the benefits SI leaders receive include increased understanding of the target course material; improved communication skills; and enhanced interaction with faculty, students, and other SI leaders and staff. They pointed out an unexpected benefit for SI leaders—proficiency in issues related to diversity. Through their SI involvement, leaders have the opportunity to interact with diverse student populations (Bidgood, 1994; Martin & Arendale, 1993a; Ramirez, 1997), which in turn, can help develop multicultural competence (Stout & McDaniel, 2006). Stout and McDaniel also found that some leaders believed that the benefits to them may even outweigh those of student participants.

According to Martin and Arendale (1993b), flexibility and openness to change and new ways of looking at things can result from leaders' adaptability in creating a session plan with multiple strategies. The experience and practice gained from being able to change learning activities to better meet the needs and demands of students in SI sessions is directly applicable to the work world, as employees are frequently asked to work as a team to solve problems. In fact, SI leaders participating in a qualitative study (Ashwin, 1993) listed increased interest by potential employers as a benefit of the experience. Having a leadership position of this kind on the student's résumé tells future employers that he/she has strong commitment and communication skills and the ability to establish positive relationships with peers as well as superiors (Stout & McDaniel, 2006).

Hurley, McKay, Scott, and James (2003) evaluated the perspective of experienced tutors who tried the SI model as part of a student-run Supplemental Instruction Project (SIP). The tutors who completed the evaluations felt their experience was positive and said they would be open to leading SIP tutorials (SI sessions) in the future. Of those who completed evaluations, 86% reported that the experience was beneficial to them on a personal level and that leading the tutorials provided a good review of the material. Similarly, in Ashwin's (1993) study of SI leaders, students noted greater understanding of course material as a benefit of the experience.

Wallace (1992) commented, "We have seen the development of these students [SI leaders] as articulate and self-assured young people" (p. 9), which indicates that SI leaders may also improve their communication skills and self-confidence. Martin and Wilcox (1996) reported that leaders increase their self-confidence as they expand their own knowledge of academic topics. By bringing increased course knowledge, communication skills, and self-confidence into their SI leadership position, they are seen by others as experienced learners. As the SI model is supported by proven learning theory, being a leader allows students to better understand the elements involved in their own approach to learning.

Conclusion

As institutions of higher learning have become increasingly student-centered, they have searched for ways to increase retention. According to Chickering and Gamson (1987), institutions that provide sufficient student-faculty contact, cooperation among students, opportunities for active learning, prompt feedback, ample time on task, high expectations, and respect for diverse talents and ways of learning are more likely to retain students. Not only is SI an academic support program that incorporates many of these recommendations, but research on SI has proven it to be an effective retention program. Numerous large- and small-scale studies conducted since SI's inception 30 years ago have demonstrated that students who attend SI experience statistically significant increases in mean final course grades and are more likely to reenroll and graduate. These results have been shown to be consistent for both prepared and at-risk students. Some studies have even shown that attending SI helps students with affective development and long-term academic achievement.

The educational community will continue to benefit from additional studies that demonstrate the impact of SI on the aforementioned areas, but there is also a need for research in many other areas. For example, the benefits SI provides for SI leaders, the effect it has on course evaluations, and the ways in which instructor pedagogy might change as a result of the communication between the SI leader and instructor are all areas of interest to SI practitioners. As an integral part of hundreds of institutions, SI has influenced myriad aspects of the educational atmosphere, but there are questions yet to be answered.

References

Arendale, D. (1996). *Frontloaded academic support: Supplemental Instruction in two-year colleges.* Unpublished manuscript, The University of Missouri – Kansas City.

Arendale, D., & Martin, D.C. (1997). *Review of research concerning the effectiveness of Supplemental Instruction from the University of Missouri – Kansas City and other institutions.* Kansas City, MO: The University of Missouri – Kansas City.

Ashwin, P. W. (1993). *Supplemental Instruction: Does it enhance the student experience of higher education?* Unpublished doctoral dissertation, Kingston University, London, England.

Astin, A. (1998). *Evaluating remedial programs is not just a methodological issue.* Keynote at Conference on Replacing Remedial Education in Higher Education at Stanford University, Palo Alto, CA.

Bidgood, P. (1994). The success of Supplemental Instruction: Statistical evidence. In C. Rust & J. Wallace (Eds.), *Helping students to learn from each other: Supplemental Instruction* (pp. 71-79). Birmingham, England: Staff and Educational Development Association.

Blanc, R. A., DeBuhr, L. E., & Martin, D. C. (1983). Breaking the attrition cycle: The effects of Supplemental Instruction on undergraduate performance and attrition. *Journal of Higher Education, 54,* 81-89.

Blanc, R. A., & Martin, D. C. (1994). Supplemental Instruction: Increasing student performance and persistence in difficult academic courses. *Academic Medicine: Journal of the Association of American Medical Colleges, 69*(6), 452-454.

Bok, D. (2006). *Our underachieving colleges: A candid look at how students learn and why they should be learning more.* Princeton, NJ: Princeton University Press.

Chickering, A.W., & Gamson, Z.F. (1987). Seven principles for good practice in undergraduate education. *AAHE Bulletin, 39*(7), 3-7.

Congos, D. H., & Schoeps, N. (2003). Inside Supplemental Instruction sessions: One model of what happens that improves grades and retention revisited. *Journal of Student Centered Learning, 1*(3), 161-172.

Dewey, J. (1916). *Democracy and education.* New York: Macmillan.

Gattis, K.W. (2000). Long-term knowledge gains due to Supplemental Instruction in college chemistry courses, *Journal of Research and Development in Education, 33*(2), 118-126.

Grubb, W. N. (1998). *Replacing remediation in higher education.* Paper presented at the National Center for Postsecondary Improvement Conference, Palo Alto, CA.

Hensen, K. A., & Shelley, M. C., II (2003). The impact of Supplemental Instruction: Results from a large, public, midwestern university. *Journal of College Student Development, 44*(2), 250-259.

Hodges, R. (2001). Encouraging high-risk student participation in tutoring and Supplemental Instruction. *Journal of Developmental Education, 24*(3), 2-11.

Hudson, W. W. (1987). Index of self-esteem (ISE). In K. Corcoran & J. Fisher (Eds.), *Measures for clinical practice: A sourcebook* (pp. 188-190). New York: Free Press.

Hurley, K .F., McKay, D. W., Scott, T. M., & James, B. M. (2003). The Supplemental Instruction project: Peer-devised and delivered tutorials. *Medical Teacher, 25*(4), 404-407.

Jones, J. P., & Fields, K. T. (2001). The role of Supplemental Instruction in the first accounting course. *Issues in Accounting Education, 16*(4), 531-547.

Kuh, G .D., Schuh, J., Witt, E., & Associates. (1991). *Involving colleges: Successful approaches to fostering student learning and development outside the classroom.* San Francisco: Jossey-Bass.

Martin, D. C. (1980). Learning centers in professional schools. In K.V. Lauridsen (Ed.). *Examining the scope of learning centers* (pp. 69-79). San Francisco: Jossey-Bass.

Martin, D. C., & Arendale, D. (1993a). Review of research on Supplemental Instruction. In D.C. Martin & D. Arendale (Eds.), *Supplemental Instruction: Improving first-year student success in high-risk courses* (Monograph No. 7, 2nd ed., pp. 19-26). Columbia, SC: University of South Carolina, The National Resource Center for The Freshman Year Experience.

Martin, D., & Arendale, D. (1993b). *Supplemental instruction: Improving first-year student success in high-risk courses* (Monograph No. 7, 2nd ed.). Columbia, SC: University of South Carolina, The National Resource Center for The Freshman Year Experience.

Martin, D.C., & Arendale, D. (Eds.). (1994). *Supplemental Instruction: Increasing achievement and retention.* (New Directions of Teaching and Learning No. 60). San Francisco: Jossey-Bass.

Martin, D. C., & Blanc, R. A. (1981). The learning center's role in retention: Integrating student support services with departmental instruction. *Journal of Developmental and Remedial Education, 4*(3), 2-4, 21-23.

Martin, D. C., Blanc, R. A., & Arendale, D. (1996). Supplemental Instruction: Supporting the classroom experience. In J.N. Hankin (Ed.), *The community college: Opportunity and access for America's first-year students* (Monograph No. 19, pp. 123-133). Columbia, SC: University of South Carolina, The National Resource Center for The Freshman Year Experience and Students in Transition.

Martin, D. C., & Wilcox, F. K. (1996). Supplemental Instruction: Helping students to help each other. In G. Wisker, & S. Brown (Eds.), *Enabling student learning: Systems and strategies* (pp. 97-101). Birmingham, England: Kogan Page Publishers and the Staff and Educational Developmental Association (SEDA).

Ogden, P., Thompson, D., Russell, A., & Simons, C. (2003). Supplemental Instruction: Short- and long-term impact. *Journal of Developmental Education, 26*(3), 2-8.

Pascarella, E. T., & Terenzini, P. T. (1991). *How college affects students: Findings and insight from twenty years of research.* San Francisco: Jossey-Bass.

Pascarella, E. T., & Terenzini, P. T. (2005). *How college affects students: A third decade of research.* San Francisco: Jossey-Bass.

Ramirez, G. M. (1997). Supplemental Instruction: The long-term impact. *Journal of Developmental Education, 21*, 2-10.

Rotter, J. B. (1976). The Rotter internal-external control scale. In E. J. Phares (Ed.), *Locus of control in personality* (pp.178-180). Morristown, NJ: General Learning Press.

Sherer, M., Maddux, J. E., Mercandante, B., Prentice-Dunn, S., Jacobs, B., & Rogers, R. W. (1987). Self-efficacy scale (SES). In K. Corcoran & J. Fisher (Eds.), *Measures for clinical practice: A sourcebook* (pp. 294-296). New York: Free Press.

Slavin, R. E. (1990). *Cooperative learning: Theory, research, and practice.* Englewood Cliffs, NJ: Prentice-Hall.

Stout, M. L. & McDaniel, A. (2006). Benefits to SI leaders. In M. E. Stone & G. Jacobs (Eds.), *New visions for Supplemental Instruction (SI): SI for the 21st century* (pp. 55-62). San Francisco: Jossey-Bass.

Tinto, V. (1993). *Leaving college: Rethinking the causes and cures of student attrition* (2nd ed.). Chicago: The University of Chicago Press.

Visor, J. N., Johnson, J. J., & Cole, L. N. (1992). The relationship of Supplemental Instruction to affect. *Journal of Developmental Education, 16*, 228-232.

Visor, J. N., Johnson, J. J., Schollaet, A. M., Good-Majah, C. A., & Davenport, O. (1995). Supplemental Instruction's impact on affect: A follow-up and expansion. *Proceedings from the 20th Annual Conference on Developmental Education* (pp. 36-37). Chicago: National Association for Developmental Education.

Wallace, J. (1992). Students helping students to learn. *The New Academic, 1*(2), 8-9.

Chapter 3

Theoretical Frameworks That Inform the Supplemental Instruction Model

Sandra Zerger

The Supplemental Instruction (SI) community uses a variety of strategies to help students learn more effectively. Over the last 35 years, the ideas of a number of theorists have informed our approach to and delivery of the SI model. However, given the dynamic and fluid nature of the model, we find that we must continually reconcile our practice to new and existing theories to ensure SI's continuing effectiveness. Beginning as a reaction to the prevalence and inadequacy of strict behaviorist learning theory, SI has integrated and, in some cases, moved beyond the views of cognitivists, learning styles theorists, social constructivists, and critical theorists.

The Changing Nature of a College Education

In *Our Underachieving Colleges,* Bok (2006) reminds us that, until the end of the 19th century, the purpose of a college education was to instill a particular mental discipline in the elite that they could then apply to other subjects. Mental discipline meant translating Latin and Greek authors and imitating their style in writing and oral recitations. Bok notes that this attitude prevailed until the end of the century when Edward Thorndike's experiments suggested that, "the skills acquired through painstaking translations of Cicero and Virgil would rarely help students to analyze and solve problems outside the realm of Latin texts" (p. 13). As long as only an elite group attended college, however, the system of a master teacher with the authority of the ancients at his back and the method of *imitatio* as his guide was the norm in higher education. It was not until the number of colleges and universities mushroomed in the mid-20th century that education was open to the masses. From 1945 to 2000, the number of BA degrees awarded in the United States rose from 157,349 to 1.2 million (Bok).

The Waning of Behaviorism

As American universities—and the number of students enrolled in them—multiplied during the 20th century, lecture replaced translation and imitation as the primary mode of instruction, a system that Barr and Tagg (1995) dub the *Instruction Paradigm*. In this paradigm, knowledge, by definition, consists of matter dispensed or delivered by an instructor... Learning is presumed to be cumulative because it amounts to ingesting more and more chunks. A degree is awarded when a student has received a specified amount of instruction (p. 21).

Within this framework, colleges must provide instruction to produce learning, but colleges that measure learning by the amount of instruction students receive are stymied in achieving the ends of education by holding on to unproductive means. Barr and Tagg suggest that the mission of colleges and universities should move away from providing instruction and toward producing learning. This shift has not yet occurred.

The Instruction Paradigm is grounded in behaviorism in that it focuses on a simplified model of learning—a predicted response (i.e., absorption of instruction) to external stimuli (i.e., lecture, syllabus, texts). Behaviorism is most often associated with the work of B. F. Skinner (1938, 1982) who argued that behavior originates as a result of external environmental stimuli, not internal psychological processes. The activity of the mind is not relevant to or necessary for explaining behavior. In other words, it is behavior not mental processes that psychology should study and discover through experimentation on organisms.

As it is applied to education, behaviorism requires that specific learning objectives be determined before administering a lesson so that students can be reinforced at the moment they demonstrate the correct behavior. Using operant conditioning, lessons (such as a text to be studied) are broken down into small parts, sometimes no longer than a paragraph. Students are prompted to respond to questions on the lesson, and their correct answers are reinforced. They are encouraged to work independently, at their own pace, and prompts from instructors decrease as the learner proceeds successfully through the material. This approach to instruction has become less desirable to educators emphasizing learner-centered instruction, primarily because it is best applied to lower-order skills, such as memorization. Teaching more sophisticated material that requires higher-order thinking skills, such as application and prediction, are not easily done with operant conditioning. These early approaches to education suggest why otherwise capable students sometimes struggled with their courses. For this reason, Deanna Martin, founder of SI, turned to other models to find strategies for helping students overcome these challenges.

SI Emphasizes Student Learning: A Cognitive Model

In an effort to discover an approach that favored learning over instruction, Martin studied the work of Bandura (1977), a researcher who began as a behaviorist but is often considered a founder of cognitivism. Bandura moved beyond behaviorism when he added the impact of behavior on environment and the interplay of imagery and language to his concept of personality. Unlike the behaviorists, cognitivists believe that observation is a powerful tool for learning because, if they are paying attention, people internalize behaviors they see modeled by storing images and verbal descriptions in their minds. If motivated to do so, individuals can then reproduce these behaviors, often very accurately. The addition of the internal processes of storing modeled behaviors allowed Bandura to theorize more effectively about how learning results from observation as opposed to the behaviorists who did not consider mental processes relevant.

For Bandura, then, modeling is key in successful instruction, and the SI model relies heavily on cognitivism in the facilitation techniques employed by SI leaders. For example, when the leader waits between asking a question and restating, rewording, or asking another question (i.e., Wait-Time 1), his/her behavior suggests to (or models for) students that it should take them some time to formulate a response. Similarly, when the SI leader allows sufficient time to pass between a response to a question and another utterance from the leader or a student (i.e., Wait-Time 2), students observe that multiple answers are desirable. Many times, use of Wait-Time 2 results in students listening to each other, not just the leader, and building on the responses of their peers (Rowe, 1987). University of Missouri – Kansas City SI trainers model appropriate leader behaviors (e.g., involving all students, planning for contingencies, challenging leaders, and encouraging students to work in groups) by conducting training workshops in the same way they expect a leader to facilitate a session.

As the cognitivists in the field of psychology were working to understand the importance of modeling, educators were trying to account for the difficulties of teaching higher-order skills with behaviorist techniques. Kolb (1984)—influenced by Dewey, Lewin, and Piaget—determined that learning occurs in a cycle, as learners (a) act in a specific situation, (b) observe and understand the effects of their action, (c) abstract general rules from the effects, and (d) apply the rules in new settings. For effective learning to occur, individuals must possess the skills necessary to complete the four stages of the learning cycle. Yet many learners find they are stronger in one or two skill areas. These strengths comprise the learning style of the individual. While Kolb's work on the learning cycle has been helpful to learner-centered education, some practitioners have taken Kolb's recommendations too literally, assuming that an individual with a certain learning style can learn only when instructed to use that skill. In addition, Morgan (2003) notes that many well-regarded educational researchers questioned the validity of Kolb's learning styles theory and the theoretical framework on which it is based.

For these reasons, the popularity of learning styles in the field of education did not influence the formation of the SI model as it exists today, although many practitioners find it of value and incorporate its core tenets in individual SI programs.

Piaget and the Evolution of the SI Model

Jean Piaget's notion of intelligence as a developmental process became a guiding influence for Martin and led to the incorporation of small-group discussion in the SI paradigm. Cognitive structures and processes, according to Piaget (1929), develop gradually as learning is constructed through the organization and integration of new information and experience. Learning is defined as the ability to abstract the physical world through mental representations of personal experiences and concepts. These representations are referred to as schemas, which develop as a result of processes called assimilation and accommodation. In assimilation, the learner brings a new object or concept into an existing schema and integrates that information into his/her existing worldview. Accommodation involves changing a schema to fit the discordant information—often changing the learner's fundamental beliefs about how the world works (Dykstra, Boyle, & Monarch, 1992). Assimilation and accommodation may result in disequilibrium that eventually leads to cognitive growth once equilibrium is restored. This is referred to as cognitive dissonance. In other words, social interaction causes conflict or feelings of discomfort, analogous to the muscle pain that results from vigorous physical activity. In order to prompt the body to build new muscle tissue, the existing tissue must first be torn. During SI sessions, when existing schemas are challenged, students may be dismayed at the loss of understanding, however insufficient or incorrect it may have been. Yet, the leader encourages them to question, discuss, and use their prior knowledge as a framework for new schemas. The group discussion allows new knowledge to emerge, and equilibrium (the absence of mental discomfort) is restored.

Constructivist Theory

Constructivists such as Geertz (1983) and Bakhtin (1986; 1993) have argued that knowledge is not time and context free; rather, it is always situated in a local context. Language and what language says—ideas, forms of truth, concrete concepts—are always the product of interactions between at least two people. Knowledge and understanding, therefore, are not constructed individually but in dialogue with others, and facts are "true" in the social context in which they were created. Related to this is social constructivist theory (Vygotsky, 1962; 1978), which maintains that human learning presupposes a specific social goal. Vygotsky defined a "zone of proximal development" as the difference between what the learner can do independently and a level of potential development the learner can reach with the guidance of a sage or in collaboration with capable peers. The experienced learner can provide support, or *scaffolding,* for the new learner, thereby boosting the new learner's abilities to the level of the experienced learner. What learners are able to do in collaboration today, they will be able to do independently in the future.

Students in SI, guided by a leader who is knowledgeable about the course content and effective learning strategies, help each other gradually move from the zone of proximal development to higher levels. As such, SI leaders are trained to emphasize the difficult concepts in the sessions and plan activities that require students to collaborate. However, the value of collaboration and group study to gaining new knowledge is not always apparent to undergraduate students. Thus, students may feel resentment when the leader redirects them to the group rather than answering their questions directly. Collaboration also involves a different skill set, and students may experience discomfort in learning or using a new skill. However, this discomfort usually decreases over time.

Other proponents of collaboration have focused on the need for students to engage in experiential learning (Dykstra, 1997; Dykstra et al., 1992), where students collectively construct their own knowledge in order to achieve conceptual understanding, rather than mere memorization. The classroom becomes a place where ideas are questioned and learning is facilitated to develop improved comprehension. Students are encouraged to work collaboratively by sharing ideas with one another and are not allowed to "get by and, in some cases, be successful by memorizing particular problem solutions and using them by rote in their attempts to solve new problems" (Dykstra et al., p. 3). The combined wisdom of the group should allow students to examine their own ideas, and their mutual experiences should help them understand new information. The solution for students is not about having quick, easy answers available, but about producing knowledge as a group rather than receiving knowledge from the instructor-expert (Dykstra, 2001).

Some scholars have addressed learning as a process of conceptual change, looking particularly at concepts that are counterintuitive to the students' everyday ideas of the world (Hynd, McNish, Lay, & Fowler, 1996; Hynd, Qian, Keith, & Lay, 1994). Their findings include the principle that students who are grappling with contradictory notions of the world fare better if they view knowledge as a connected set of complex concepts rather than simple, isolated facts. Yet, Vygotsky (1987) suggests students may have trouble learning counterintuitive concepts, because "the child's spontaneous concepts develop from below to above, from the more elementary and lower characteristics to the higher, while his scientific concepts develop from above to below, from the more complex and higher characteristics to the more elementary" (p. 219). In other words, the cognitive processes for everyday concepts and scientific ones differ, and the scientific processes do not conform to our everyday notions.

However, students can learn counterintuitive concepts by experiencing conflict (disequilibrium), investigating differences between prior notions and scientific explanations, building bridges to new concepts (often through analogies), being helped to see the usefulness of these concepts, examining texts with corroborating or refutable information, building concept maps, tying the concepts to the big picture, working in groups, and talking to one another. These are all practices that have been incorporated into the SI model.

Social Interdependence Theory and Cooperative Learning

First studied in the early 1900s by Koffka, one of the founders of the Gestalt school of psychology, social interdependence theory has since been refined by scholars who were influenced by the constructivists. Initially, psychologists interested in group interactions believed that people working together form dynamic, interdependent wholes because they share common goals (Lewin, 1935, 1938). When the members of the group perceive that their goals can be achieved only if the other members also accomplish their goals (interdependence), this affects the social interaction of the group and, ultimately, the outcomes. In cooperative situations, the interdependence is positive, so members will substitute actions of another for their own, invest psychological energy in actions outside themselves, and remain open to influence from others in the group. If the actions of some members of the group impact other members, but are not reciprocal, the group is dependent, not interdependent. This results in activity in which members compete, attempting to defeat each other's efforts. If the ability for individuals to achieve their goals is unrelated to other group members' success or failure, people will perform individualistically, ignoring each other's endeavors to achieve their goals (Deutsch & Krauss,1965; Johnson & Johnson, 1989).

Johnson and Johnson (1989) and Johnson, Johnson, and Holubec (1994) applied this theory to education and found that when groups were given tasks that were structured to create positive interdependence, promotive interaction (i.e., members communicate support for each other's attempts to achieve goals) occurred. After an exhaustive meta-analysis of almost 100 years of research conducted on social interdependence, Johnson and Johnson found that individuals who participated in cooperative learning performed about 66% better than the average person learning through a competitive or individualistic method. Although these results suggest that cooperative learning is a fundamentally sound approach to education, it is essential that the tasks assigned to cooperative learning groups are designed so that each individual is participating. If a few members perform the majority of the work, the group becomes negatively interdependent and does not experience the benefits associated with cooperative learning.

Martin designed the SI model to encourage positive interdependence among group members. Common session activities such as note review (students read aloud from lecture notes in turn so that everyone leaves with a complete set), matrices (students organize material and then compare organizational frameworks), and divide and conquer (students work in small groups on portions of material and then gather to share results) are structured so that each learner contributes to the common goal of the group: reviewing and understanding difficult course material. When SI leaders are not trained to implement these strategies, are not observed regularly, and experience resistance from students, they often alter these strategies so that the activities become competitive or individualistic because such interactions result in less resistance from students. The real benefit of cooperative learning cannot be underestimated, but neither can it be taken for granted by SI supervisors, who are responsible for training and observing SI leaders regularly.

Critical Theory

Critical theory, as it has evolved in the social sciences, seeks not only to describe history or culture but also to influence change as a result of newfound understanding (McCarthy, 1991). In education, Freire (1993/1972), a Brazilian theorist, has used this approach to illuminate the oppression of people by pedagogical practice. Freire asserts that much of modern education is based on a banking system: The expert deposits knowledge into the learner. This model emphasizes and reinforces social inequities and results in a learning "culture of silence." Instead, Freire recommends a respectful dialogue between learners as a method to effect social change and to position education within the lived experience of the learner. Good pedagogy empowers learners to take control of their own learning process. This can be seen in the SI model. The essence of the learning that takes place in SI sessions is the interaction and conversation that students share as they construct knowledge, and the informal atmosphere seeks to reproduce how students might socialize and study together outside organized academic support. Because SI is offered to all students in supported courses and each student must contribute to the session, success becomes accessible to all learners.

A learning model created to retain students in the health sciences, SI always has been about access to learning for all students. One evolution of the model has demonstrated how SI can provide disadvantaged students with the means for success. Glen Jacobs (personal communication, February 15, 2006), executive director of the International Center for SI, has reported how SI has been used in post-apartheid South Africa to help the masses from undereducated environments succeed in the newly integrated institutions of higher education. That is, SI often becomes a bridge between disadvantaged schools and the university. Zerger, Clark-Unite, and Smith (2006) note that SI has become a vehicle for transformation in South Africa, both to support new students entering the universities and to train and develop faculty. Faculty indicated that after attending the SI training workshops, they have adapted their teaching methods to include SI's more interactive and collaborative methods. In comments at the Third International Conference on SI in Boston, Deanna Martin (2004) argued for the use of SI to empower learners to take control of their own learning and that learning should have as its goal, liberation, rather than domination—which argues for SI as a form of social justice.

Conclusion

To truly understand how and why Supplemental Instruction is effective, it is crucial to understand the learning theories upon which it is based. The SI community of scholars has shaped, through practice, this theoretical framework. As evidenced in this chapter, SI has borrowed from a multitude of learning theorists, and then adapted these ideas to work in conjunction with one another. Supplemental Instruction has taken from the behaviorists the concepts of modeling and positive reinforcement and the practice of breaking complex tasks into their more digestible component parts. From the cognitive developmentalists, SI has adopted the ideas of accommodation and assimilation, schemas, and cognitive dissonance. The constructivists have contributed the concepts of scaffolding and collaboration and the premise that knowledge is produced rather than distributed. The SI model has also been informed by the critical theorists who advocate for learners to be empowered to take an active role in their own learning processes, thus overcoming the "culture of silence" often found in education. From the cognitivists to the critical theorists, these theories provide continuity and support for the myriad forms of SI that cover the globe.

References

Bakhtin, M. M. (1986). *Speech genres and other late essays*. (V. W. McGee, Trans: C. Emerson & M. Holquist, Eds.). Austin, TX: University of Texas Press.

Bakhtin, M. M. (1993). *Toward a philosophy of the act*. (V. Liapuno, Trans.: M. Holquist, & V. Liapunov, Eds.). Austin, TX: University of Texas Press.

Bandura, A. (1977). *Social learning theory*. Englewood Cliffs, NJ: Prentice Hall.

Barr, R. B., & Tagg, J. (1995). From teaching to learning—A new paradigm for undergraduate education. *Change, 27*(6), 13-25. Retrieved November 30, 2006, from http://critical.tamucc.edu/~blalock/readings/tch2learn.htm

Bok, D. (2006). *Our underachieving colleges: A candid look at how much students learn and why they should be learning more*. Princeton, NJ: Princeton University Press.

Deutsch, M., & Krauss, R. (1965). *Theories in social psychology*. New York: Basic Books.

Dykstra, D. (1997). The role of scientific terminology in research and teaching: Is something important missing? *Journal of Research in Science Teaching, 34*(6), 655-660.

Dykstra, D. (2001). *Some possible misunderstandings of the philosophy*. Retrieved February 20, 2006, from http://www.boisestate.edu/physics/dykstra/muphil.html

Dykstra, D. I., Boyle, C. F., & Monarch, I. (1992). Studying conceptual change in learning physics. *Science Education, 76*(6), 615-652.

Freire, P. (1993). *Pedagogy of the oppressed*. (M. B. Ramos, Trans.). New York: Continuum. (Originally published in English in 1972)

Geertz, C. (1983). *Local knowledge: Further essays in interpretive anthropology*. New York: Basic Books.

Hynd. C. R., McNish, M., Lay, K., & Fowler, P. (1996). High school physics: The role of text in learning counterintuitive information. *Reading Research Report No. 46*. National Reading Research Project of the University of Georgia and the University of Maryland.

Hynd, C. R., Qian, G., Keith, M., & Lay, K. (1994). Learning counterintuitive physics concepts: The effects of text and educational environment. *Reading Research Report No. 16*. National Reading Research Project of the University of Georgia and the University of Maryland.

Johnson, D., W., & Johnson, R. T. (1989). Social skills for successful group work. *Educational Leadership, 47*(4), 29-33.

Johnson, D. W., Johnson, R. T., & Holubec, E. J. (1994). *The nuts and bolts of cooperative learning*. Edina, MN: Interaction Book.

Kolb, D. A. (1984). *Experiential learning: Experience as the source of learning and development*. Englewood Cliff, NJ: Prentice-Hall.

Lewin, K. (1935). *A dynamic theory of personality; selected papers*. (D. K. Adams & K. E. Zener, Trans.). New York: McGraw Hill.

Martin, D. C. (2004, June). *Supplemental Insturction (SI): Past, present, and future*. A welcome address delivered at the 3rd International SI Conference, Boston, MA.

Lewin, K. (1938). *The conceptual representation and the measurement of psychological forces*. Durham, NC: Duke University Press.

McCarthy, T. (1991). *Ideals and illusions: On reconstruction and deconstruction in contemporary critical theory*. Cambridge: The MIT Press.

Morgan, H. (2003). *Real learning: A bridge to cognitive neuroscience*. Lanham, MD: Scarecrow Education.

Piaget, J. (1929). *The child's conception of the world*. New York: Harcourt, Brace Jovanovich.

Rowe, M. B. (1987). Wait time: Slowing down may be a way of speeding up. *American Educator, 47*, 38-43.

Skinner, B. F. (1938). *The behavior of organisms.* New York: Appleton-Century.

Skinner, B. F. (1982). *Skinner for the classroom: Selected essays.* (R. Epstein, Ed.). Champaign, IL: Research Press.

Vygotsky, L. S. (1962). *Thought and language.* Cambridge, MA: MIT Press.

Vygotsky, L. S. (1978). *Mind in society: The development of higher psychological processes.* (A. R. Luria, M. Lopez-Morillas, & M. Cole, Trans.: M. Cole, V. John-Steiner, S. Scribner, & E. Souberman, Eds.). Cambridge, MA: Harvard University Press. (Original chapters published in 1930 and 1935)

Vygotsky, L. S. (1987). *The collected works of L. S. Vygotsky. Vol. 1: Problems of general psychology.* (N. Minick, Trans.: R. W. Rieber, & A. S. Carton, Eds.). New York: Plenum.

Zerger, S., Clark-Unite, C., & Smith, L. (2006). How Supplemental Instruction (SI) benefits faculty, administration, and institutions. In M. E. Stone & G. Jacobs (Eds.), *Supplemental Instruction: New visions for empowering student learning* (New Directions for Teaching and Learning, No. 106, p. 63-72). San Francisco: Jossey-Bass.

Chapter 4

Implementing a New Supplemental Instruction Program

F. Kim Wilcox

As an academic support program, Supplemental Instruction (SI) works best when it is carefully constructed in a patient and unhurried manner. Beginning any academic program with patience is challenging because support programs are typically adopted with a sense of urgency. When we identify problems, our tendency is to rush to discover their solutions, apply the fixes, and then hope for instant results. Such approaches, however, are not likely to yield long-term solutions. Successful, long-term support programs are the result of deliberately building an infrastructure with enough flexibility to accommodate the particulars of specific settings and courses.

SI's longevity as an academic support program is due, in part, to its natural fluidity and adaptability. It has core principles but not a single, static, and rigid process for implementation and administration. This chapter will discuss how to lay the foundation for a successful SI program by remaining flexible, selecting suitable courses, inviting faculty to participate, selecting and training qualified supervisors and leaders, realistically estimating time and resource requirements, regularly assessing and reporting program results, and expanding responsibly.

Flexibility: A Healthy Start

One of the core principles of SI is that it strives to provide a structure where learners develop critical thinking skills (Johnson, Johnson, & Smith, 1991) and become empowered to take ownership of knowledge. SI begins where mere memorization is abandoned in favor of true understanding. Faculty have sometimes expressed concern that SI sessions—without the benefit of faculty members' presence to correct mistakes—might lead the group to collective misunderstanding. It is a valid concern but must be weighed against the misinformation that develops when then learners are never permitted to take ownership of the content of the discipline. Just as students should be allowed to make mistakes that lead to increased understanding, SI programs should also begin with the freedom to make mistakes because mistakes frequently foster innovation.

Further, as each institution develops its program, it will be faced with numerous decisions about how closely to follow the traditional model. There are no easy answers here, but, having faced this issue with SI adopters in 29 countries and over as many years, we have learned that, all things considered, flexibility is preferable to rigidity. Programs that are housed in institutions and directed by supervisors who are willing to consider variations on the model are typically healthier than those that are locked into an overly prescriptive formula. Flexibility creates breathing space to make necessary changes where unique situations dictate them, and it allows the freedom to return to convention where modification does not lead to greater success. Thus, this chapter does not offer a blueprint for starting an SI program, but rather offers guidance for institutions to find their own ways toward building a successful program.

Developing a Pilot Program

One of the first decisions a new program adopter must make is who to approach first: college administrators who must approve and fund SI or faculty whose courses and students will be supported by SI. Both faculty and administrators are more likely to support a program when the other has already endorsed it (Light, 1990). Administrators may hesitate to fund a program for which faculty have not voiced support, and faculty members are unlikely to invest time and energy in something that has no funding allocation from administration. Supervisors will, of course, want to consider the working and/ or personal relationships they have with each group, but, all things being equal, attempting to work with both groups simultaneously is the safest approach. Supervisors will likely get a better response from both when each knows that the other is in the loop, even if neither is completely on board.

As supervisors approach faculty and administrators, they should keep in mind that each group may have a slightly different stake or interest in the issues surrounding academic support. SI tends to be popular with administrators because it is proven to reduce attrition and improve the graduation rates of students while being more cost-effective than traditional tutoring. Nevertheless, supervisors may face administrator resistance when applying for new budget lines for SI. Faculty members support SI when they believe it will increase student learning and assist students in meeting the academic and curricular requirements of the course. However, they may hesitate to adopt SI in their courses if they perceive that it will create additional work for them or somehow compromise the manner in which they teach their course. Both faculty and administration may initially reject SI, simply because they have a well-developed and healthy skepticism about new programs.

Given the understandable reluctance of both faculty and administrators to adopt new programs, a logical first step would be a pilot. Piloting SI will provide faculty members with the freedom to experiment with and witness the actual results of attaching SI to their courses. Not requiring faculty to make a final decision for or against the program until after the pilot will give them time to gather information about how SI actually works in their individual courses—rather than relying on solely theoretical arguments. Administrators are also more likely to approve a pilot than commit to funding a program about which they are unsure. Starting with a smaller, limited number of courses also has the added benefit of providing the SI supervisor with more time to actually learn how SI will work on an individual campus and in specific courses. It also allows more time for all involved to suggest recommendations for changes as the program develops.

Program Staffing

In an academic support program such as SI, the success of the program is determined by the people involved. It is essential that all of the players be thoughtfully selected, trained, and supported. Typically in SI, there are four groups of individuals who work together to contribute to the program's success: (a) the SI supervisor (sometimes supported by additional program staff), (b) the SI leaders, (c) the faculty members whose courses are supported, and (d) the students who attend. In most cases, the SI supervisor is also the program coordinator, though as programs grow, there is often the need to add additional supervisors to help observe sessions and mentor SI leaders. These individuals can be other staff members, faculty, and/or experienced SI leaders.

Supervisor Training, Time Commitment, and Responsibility

A solid foundation for implementing SI includes training SI supervisors and leaders. It is impossible to distill the collaborative and interactive spirit of the SI model into a written manual; rather, supervisors and leaders both should attend training workshops in order to interact with their peers and process information using the SI model. This serves to ensure true learning while simultaneously reinforcing the supervisor's endorsement of the model, especially if he/she is new to the program. Collaborating with peers also helps supervisors thoroughly research all aspects of program development, investigate the successes and failures that others may have already encountered, and avoid their mistakes.

Typically the person who will be the SI supervisor conducts the training workshop for the leaders. Training for supervisors, however, can only be obtained from the University of Missouri – Kansas City (UMKC) certified trainers. UMKC has been conducting SI supervisor workshops for the past 25 years. The supervisor training sessions include detailed discussions and exercises regarding the following topics: theoretical frameworks underlying the SI model, procedures for selecting SI courses and SI leaders, ongoing training and supervision of SI leaders, effective learning strategies and SI session activities, and evaluation and funding of the program. Although this chapter highlights the information provided in these workshops, it is not able to cover it with the same depth, nor is it a substitute for the opportunity to interact with colleagues from other campuses and UMKC trainers at a workshop.

Another critical component for the long-term health of a new initiative is an accurate estimate of the time and work required to run a successful program. A frequently asked question of new SI supervisors is how many courses they can reasonably support each semester. A pilot will provide the best information for answering that question. In general, however, supervisors should expect to spend 5-10 hours preparing for the SI leader training workshop. The training itself should be 8-16 hours, broken down into two or three sessions. For supervising and supporting leaders during the term, supervisors should allow seven to eight hours *per course, per week* for the first three weeks of the term. Although sessions usually do not start until the second week of classes, the supervisor will be busy the first week attending lectures to help leaders distribute and collect surveys (to help ascertain when students are available to meet for SI); being present in the office to answer questions from leaders; helping leaders tally surveys, recover from botched first-day speeches, and relate to faculty and students; and providing any other support necessary to prevent leaders from feeling overwhelmed. Supervisors will also begin working with SI leaders during this time to plan the first sessions for each course.

During the second and third weeks of the term—once sessions have been scheduled, assigned rooms, and are underway—the supervisor should observe and debrief the first three sessions of each leader. Leader habits and student expectations of SI are set during these critical sessions, and they can have a lasting impact on the rate of attendance, quality of student-to-student interaction, and leader confidence. Missing the opportunity to guide planning and observe, encourage, and correct facilitation during this period can mean spending the rest of the semester trying to change poor habits.

After the first few weeks, supervisors can expect to observe leaders once a week for the remainder of the first half of the term and once every other week for the second half of the term (about 2 to 3 hours of observation/debriefing per course per week for the rest of the semester). Supervisors should also continue to help leaders plan sessions on an as-needed basis (e.g., many leaders need help planning review sessions); meet with each course instructor at least once per term; research, plan, and conduct ongoing training meetings; track, file, and enter attendance data from participation logs; maintain copies of necessary forms for leaders; schedule rooms for review sessions; and be present in the office to interact with leaders during office hours. Finally, SI supervisors will need to allow time for informal interactions with SI leaders. Chatting informally with leaders allows supervisors to get to know their leaders, and this personal touch will encourage leaders to visit the office more often, talk to the supervisor when they are having trouble, and share their successes.

Based on the time commitments outlined above, it quickly becomes clear that one supervisor cannot successfully manage more than three or four leaders without some assistance. For that reason, we suggest that an SI pilot begin with no more than one course. Rather than beginning at or above the maximum possible for one supervisor, starting with only one course allows for a period of program adjustment.

Selecting and Training SI Leaders

Typically, SI leaders will make a commitment of 10 to 15 hours each week to the SI program. SI leaders are expected to attend every course meeting (with the exception of labs); plan and conduct the regular SI sessions as well as additional, longer exam-reviews; meet with their instructor and supervisor on a weekly or bi-weekly basis; attend ongoing trainings (usually one hour every other week); and be present for one or more office hours every week. Three 50-minute sessions each week are recommended, with at least one two-hour review prior to each exam. Offering three sessions per week allows the opportunity for most students to attend at least one of the sessions and provides enough face-time (contact hours) to keep up with the most important and difficult material presented in the lecture(s).

In addition to the time requirements, SI leaders must have instructor approval, adequate content knowledge, excellent interpersonal skills, and availability to attend the course lecture and all training sessions. The inability of students to satisfy these requirements can significantly limit the pool of candidates. It can be tempting, therefore, to make exceptions on any one of the above requirements, but doing so can risk the efficacy of the program, so it is strongly discouraged.

Once a supervisor has selected leaders, the next step is to plan and conduct a preterm training workshop. Because it is not possible to give leaders all of the information they will need for the entire semester in one session, the initial training workshop should have only the following objectives:

1. *Providing leaders with the history of SI and its efficacy.* Trainers can use the material to model learning strategies.
2. *Introducing leaders to collaborative learning as participants and facilitators.* Trainers should model strategies and require participants to facilitate simulated sessions using those strategies.
3. *Preparing leaders to introduce SI on the first day of class.* Trainers should discuss the SI leader's role in the classroom and how they should relate to students and professors and offer the opportunity to practice first day speeches.
4. *Guiding leaders in the planning of sessions.* Trainers should provide the planning rubric and offer guidance on its use (See chapter appendix).
5. *Encouraging leaders to bond with each other through team-building exercises.* The training workshop should offer the opportunity to work in groups, make use of icebreaker activities, and share meals.

Additional topics such as discipline-specific strategies, potential problems, or planning review sessions should be reserved for ongoing training sessions held during the semester. (For more information about training leaders, see chapter 5 in this monograph.)

Aligning With Instructors and Selecting Courses

SI is most effective when it targets courses that students perceive to be difficult. Sometimes, courses are challenging because of the instructors who teach them. Most of the time, however, it is the curriculum itself that makes a course difficult. When selecting a course in which to pilot SI, the ideal situation is to start by choosing an historically difficult course that is taught by a rigorous yet student-friendly instructor.

Building Instructor Relationships

SI supervisors must understand that, practically speaking, SI is attached to courses at the invitation of the faculty who teach them. While it is possible to imagine a situation where SI is attached to a course because of an administrative dictate, it is unlikely that SI will find lasting success under those circumstances. Long-term quality relationships between faculty members and SI supervisors ensure successful programs. Many times, SI supervisors are hesitant to approach faculty about targeting their courses. They are concerned that faculty might feel singled out or that assigning SI to their classes might be taken as an indication that their teaching is substandard. It is sometimes easy to blame the professor for poor student academic performance, and faculty can, understandably, become defensive about this issue. The mission of SI is to support not evaluate teaching. Thus, it is important to communicate two facts to the faculty. First, SI is designed to support faculty efforts to maintain high standards in their classes while helping students meet the expectations of the course. It is not designed to water down course content to improve student grades. Second, SI is not an alternative to classroom instruction. The SI supervisor needs to communicate that the primary mission of SI is to support instruction, not to replace it. SI leaders are trained to process, not deliver, course content, and they will find themselves limited in what they can do if they violate this aspect of the model. SI is, in fact, most powerful when it is attached to outstanding instruction and may flounder if that component is missing.

Once faculty have been recruited to participate, SI supervisors find that regular communication with faculty is an important investment in the program's success. For example, supervisors should make in-person, informal visits to faculty at least once a semester and demonstrate a willingness to address their concerns, even if doing so strays a bit from the SI model. Moreover, supervisors should offer prompt data reports regarding the effectiveness of SI sessions attached to the target course. Such communication helps encourage faculty support for the program, and supervisors need faculty to demonstrate their support because students tend to value what their faculty value and disregard as unimportant those things which their faculty do not support (Visor, Johnson, & Cole, 1992). When faculty move beyond the mere acceptance of SI in their courses and actually become advocates for the program, it will be well on its way to functioning at a very high level.

Selecting Courses

While no one course or discipline is an automatic candidate for SI (or, conversely, automatically a bad candidate), some implementations of SI appear to work particularly well. For example, SI sessions connected to the natural sciences (e.g., biology, chemistry, physics) historically seem to thrive, as do pairings with other fundamental courses, such as those in history, psychology, accounting, and philosophy. While the model generally advocates SI for courses in which the class size is large and the rate of Ds, Fs, and withdrawals exceeds 30% (Martin & Arendale, 1994), sometimes, courses in which the failure/withdrawal rates may not sound any alarms might still be good candidates for SI. An example of this would be gatekeeper courses for certain majors that have additional competency requirements to advance or be accepted into a program. Although these courses are typically small, the course is so important to the students' future success in the degree program that sessions tend to be well-attended.

In addition to determining whether a course is high-risk (i.e., a DFW rate of 30% or greater), it is also helpful to know as much background information as possible about the course. Following is a list of questions that should be asked about each targeted course:

1. What courses are prerequisites for the targeted course?
2. Is the course preparatory for a professional exam?
3. How difficult do students perceive the course to be?
4. What are the course requirements?
5. Is the course taught by the same faculty member each term?
6. Are there typically teaching assistants attached to the course?
7. Is there a mandatory lab section attached?

This list is not exhaustive, and each institution or department may have more specific issues for consideration. What follows is a discussion of special circumstances that might impact the effectiveness of SI.

The best indicator of courses to target for SI may be students' perception of the course difficulty, which is directly linked to their willingness to attend SI sessions (Martin & Arendale, 1994). When students believe that courses should not be difficult, they are less likely to invest time attending SI sessions. This may be the case for SI sessions offered in developmental courses, which are not always well attended—even when such courses have high rates of unsuccessful completion. Because many developmental courses already have a review component (Tomlinson, 1989), students may be unwilling to attend sessions they perceive as more of the same, especially when the course is noncredit bearing. Some institutions, however, have found tremendous success in attaching SI to these courses, typically by modifying SI in some way (e.g., requiring attendance at SI sessions as part of the overall requirements for the course, offering extra credit for SI attendance).

Another important consideration is the nature of the course or discipline. Courses that are more *process* rather than *content* driven (e.g., English composition courses) may present difficulties for SI, predominantly because these courses are structured to allow considerable in-class time for processing material. Thus, students do not perceive a need to attend additional sessions focused on process. Additionally, students in writing courses are often working on different topics, making it difficult for the leader to plan effective collaborative activities.

Finally, courses structured as multiple, small sections with different instructors pose serious difficulties for SI leaders. Because the individual sections are small, administrators are tempted to support several sections with one leader in order to boost session size into the ideal range (5-15 students). This is in direct conflict with the SI model, however, because a leader cannot possibly attend every lecture for every section. When students do not see their leader in class on a regular basis, they are likely to forget sessions are available, forget the time or location of sessions, be uninformed if there is a scheduling change, and be less confident in the leader's knowledge of their specific course. In addition, when students from multiple sections come together in SI sessions, they may not be working on the same material at the same time. Even if the material is the same, the instruction is often very different. This puts too much pressure on the leader to know the style of each instructor and the pace of each section and is a sure-fire recipe for disaster. The end result is that SI sessions quickly take on the form of traditional one-on-one tutoring. The better plan would be to assign a different SI leader to each section of a targeted course, yet few programs have the resources to do this. Supervisors will want to consider all these issues in selecting courses, especially pilot courses, for SI.

Providing for the Program: Funding, Materials, and Facilities

The salaries for session leaders is a primary expense for SI programs, and it is an easy mistake to think about budgeting for SI solely in these terms. However, the actual cost of targeting a course with SI will require funding for training, resource materials, salary or release time for the SI supervisor(s), and other expenses. A realistic budget should reflect these expenses when the program is first initiated.

Various schools handle the compensation of SI leaders differently. While final determinations of SI leaders' salaries might be based on hourly rates and good faith estimates of number of hours worked, a stipend agreement that is fixed at the beginning of the semester is usually a simpler and more satisfying approach for both SI leaders and SI supervisors. An SI leader's responsibilities can vary from week to week, and keeping track of time cards, as well as knowing what to report and not report, can be problematic and time consuming. Most institutions report that SI leaders usually exceed expectations in the manner and time commitments with which they do their jobs. Treating SI leaders as semi-professionals will most likely result in more, not less, productivity and will avoid the difficulties of trying to clarify precisely what should or should not be included in the hourly time-sheet reports completed on a weekly basis.

Across institutions, the amount of the SI leader's salary can range anywhere from a few hundred to several thousand dollars per semester. The variations are usually, but not always, a result of regional considerations (e.g., the cost of living, competition with outside employment opportunities). Generally, SI programs arrive at a salary by estimating the average weekly time requirements of the SI leader (10-15 hours per week) and multiplying it by an applied hourly rate.

SI leader training can also be a considerable expense. Most institutions provide two days of initial training for each SI leader, which means they should budget for lunches, training materials, and other related expenses. While providing food at training is not required, it is a fairly inexpensive method of team-building because it relaxes the atmosphere and prevents leaders from going their separate ways for lunch on their own. Besides the cost of initial training, there will also be expenses associated with ongoing training for SI leaders throughout the semester.

SI leaders may also require resources/materials for their sessions. This includes items such as handouts for SI participants, poster sheets, markers, advertising and promotional items, and textbooks. We do not recommend asking professors for desk copies of the textbook. It creates additional work for them, and we have discovered that textbook publishers are reluctant to provide textbooks for tutors or SI leaders. Often if the leader has just completed the course, he or she will already have the text(s). If not, the program will need to budget the cost of providing the SI leader with a textbook for the class.

Beyond the expenses related to paying, training, and supporting SI leaders, a realistic budget must also reflect the actual or release time costs of the SI supervisor's salary. If salary funding and/or staffing time is limited, experienced SI leaders can provide a relatively inexpensive source of labor and expertise to assist in the day-to-day operations of the program. A program that is considering targeting 20 courses each term should consider hiring 23 students—20 leaders and 3 mentors (experienced leaders who assist in supervision). The most commonly underestimated time requirement of an SI program is the observation of sessions. Programs that depend on full-time staff for every aspect of the program might find themselves with an overworked staff or cutting corners that will only serve to undermine the overall quality of the program.

Although most institutions provide facilities for the SI program (e.g., rooms for training, individual sessions, and an office for leaders) at no charge, there can be significant competition for suitable rooms for the preterm training workshop. If not scheduled early, the supervisor may be forced to pay a fee to use nearby, off-campus facilities. Reserving a location several months in advance will help eliminate this potential cost. Most SI sessions will be held in regular campus classrooms, and there should be no charge for their use. Scheduling sessions in a learning center is not advisable because students may perceive the center as remedial and avoid it.

Marketing

Initial marketing efforts for SI should include cost-effective, primarily in-house measures that can reach a maximum number of students. The very best marketing tools are the SI leaders themselves because they attend every class, largely for the purpose of remaining a visible source of support to the students. Selecting leaders who have good people skills and who can relate to the students at their level will reduce formal marketing needs. Some ways to ensure that leaders are promoting SI to their students in every way possible are (a) requiring them to put the session information on the board at every class meeting, (b) asking them to make themselves more noticeable in class by being friendly and approachable and periodically sitting in a different part of the classroom, (c) suggesting that they send reminder e-mails regarding SI to the students of the class on a semi-regular basis, and (d) encouraging the facilitation of productive SI sessions. Some leaders may even be interested in forming an SI student organization. The supervisor will most likely need to serve as a sponsor, and the student members can organize a variety of activities on campus. Getting students involved informally will increase visibility of the program, and many students are looking for opportunities to serve in organizations that they can then list on their résumés.

Additionally, it is quite inexpensive to create in-house flyers that can be copied and posted throughout campus. Another common tool is bookmarks that are designed with the specifics for each SI session (e.g., SI leader's name and contact information, session times and places, test review dates, and other pertinent information regarding a particular course) for the leader to distribute in class. Other institutions have had success by having the student and/or local newspapers write an awareness article on the program, advertising on their own or on various departmental web sites, and/or promoting SI by hosting a table at campus events. All of these can be very inexpensive ways of getting the word out about a new (or existing) SI program.

Assessment

The best time to think about assessment of SI is during the planning and initiation phase of the program. There are a number of reasons why assessment is important to the longevity of SI. The most obvious one is that the SI supervisor needs to know what is happening in each SI-supported course from semester to semester and year to year. Data should be collected on how many sessions were offered, which students from the targeted courses actually attended, how often students attended, the average size of the session, and the mean final course grade and percentage of DFW rates of SI and non-SI participants. By requiring students to sign in to each session and requesting the final course grades from the registrar's office, supervisors will have all the data necessary for basic SI assessment. Collecting these data can lay the foundation for more sophisticated measurements including demographic analysis, reenrollment and graduation rates, and correlations between students' SI attendance and other predictors of academic performance such as SAT or ACT scores.

Another need for assessment is to foster credibility. Administrators and faculty are less likely to take SI seriously when no attempt is made by the SI supervisory staff to consistently collect and report data on the program. This can be important because when the inevitable funding and budgetary issues surface, programs that have only anecdotal data or internal reasoning to support their claims are most vulnerable to cutbacks or elimination.

When it comes to collecting and analyzing data, an important factor in the success of the assessment process is the degree to which supervisors actually have time to collect and analyze data. An initial proposal should include, as part of the budget, sufficient release time for collecting, entering, and analyzing data or a request for a support person to assist with this task. Program evaluation is critical to the long-term success of the program and cannot be neglected by supervisors.

Expansion of SI Program

Once an SI pilot meets with success, program administrators often are eager to expand the program. As we caution supervisors to start small, we also recommend slow expansion. Supervisors should take the time to ensure any faculty invited to participate in SI are highly supportive and understand their contribution to the model. It may be simplest to add SI courses one department at a time, and adhering to this guideline would help limit expansion to a reasonable rate of one or two courses per semester. Supervisors should keep in mind the recommendation, however, that once the program employs more than four leaders, they will need at least part-time assistance to supervise the leaders. Neglecting session observations and debriefings due to rapid expansion will quickly detract from the quality of the program, but is avoidable with proper planning.

Conclusion

Institutions planning to implement an SI program are in good company; new programs begin every term around the world. In order to set a solid foundation for a new program, the institution must identify a need to retain students, decide where the program will be situated—academic or student affairs—select as a supervisor one who is dedicated and flexible, send that individual to a training workshop at UMKC, and provide sufficient release time for the supervisor and funding for the leader salaries and necessary program materials. The supervisor should select courses to support based on the rate of unsuccessful enrollments and other relevant factors. Students who are content-competent, possess excellent interpersonal skills, available to attend the course lecture, and flexible in their own course schedule will make outstanding SI leaders. A successful preterm leader training workshop will prepare leaders for the first day of class, while also introducing the history of SI, effective collaborative learning strategies, and planning of SI sessions. If not assessed on a regular basis, pilots will likely not secure repeat funding, and careful attendance records are the basis of all program evaluation. Lastly, programs should be expanded slowly to ensure continued quality. Flexibility is key, however. While this chapter has provided guidelines for developing programs, it is important to note that institutions must design their SI programs to serve the unique needs of their students/campuses.

References

Johnson, D. W., Johnson, R. T., & Smith, K. A. (1991). *Cooperative learning: Increasing college faculty instructional productivity.* (ASHE-ERIC Higher Education Report No. 4). Washington, DC: The George Washington University.

Light, R. J. (1990). *The Harvard assessment seminars: Explorations with students and faculty about teaching, learning, and student life.* Cambridge, MA: Harvard University.

Martin, D. C., & Arendale, D. (Eds.). (1994). *Supplemental Instruction: Increasing achievement and retention* (New Directions for Teaching and Learning No. 60). San Francisco: Jossey-Bass.

Tomlinson, L. M. (1989). *Postsecondary developmental programs: A traditional agenda with new imperatives.* (ASHE-ERIC Higher Education Report No. 3). Washington, DC: The George Washington University.

Visor, J. N., Johnson, J. J., & Cole, L. N. (1992). The relationship of Supplemental Instruction to affect. *Journal of Developmental Education, 16*(2), 12-18.

Appendix

SI Session Planning Rubric

Session Date & Day of Week _____ **SI Leader** _____

Course_____ **Course Instructor**_____

Objective: What are the one or two most difficult concepts that the students need to work on today?

_____

_____

_____

Beginning reminders:
1.   Arrange seats in a circle
2.   Hand out Participation Log
3.   Set agenda with group
4.   Remember to relax and be flexible!

Content to Cover:	**Processes to Use:***

Possible processes to use: Informal Quiz, Matrix, Reciprocal Questioning, Paired Problem Solving, Turn to Your Partner, Note Processing, Problem Solving Rubric, Formal Definitions (or ID's), Text Review (Divide and Conquer), Pictorial Representations, Sequencing

Possible closure techniques: Predict next lecture, summarize session, informal quiz, one-minute writing

After session comments/thoughts:

_____

_____

_____

Chapter 5

Recruiting and Training Supplemental Instruction Leaders

Amelia McDaniel

Every semester, Supplemental Instruction (SI) supervisors around the world spend countless hours searching for qualified leaders. Because SI leaders hold a unique position in the classroom, many supervisors find they spend more time explaining to their applicants what leaders do not do, rather than what they do. They are neither instructors nor students, neither teaching assistants nor tutors. Rather, SI leaders are model learners to whom students can look for guidance in the course.

Although SI is a highly specialized area of education, most people outside the field understand it as a tutoring program. Therefore, when searching for resources to help build a leader training program, many supervisors find themselves relying on the same principles or activities that they use to train tutors. While this will provide leaders with the skills they need in one-on-one encounters with students, in general, training based on tutoring models will leave leaders lacking the tools they need to plan session activities, manage large groups of students, and model good learning behaviors. These are practices that many primary and secondary teachers are taught in teacher education programs, so it may be more helpful to borrow from their approach for training SI leaders to perform these tasks successfully.

This chapter discusses strategies for developing a customized set of SI leader qualifications, recruiting SI leader applicants, selecting qualified candidates through a three-phase application process, and organizing formal preterm and ongoing training sessions. This chapter also explores how regularly observing and debriefing SI sessions can serve as valuable training for leaders.

Customizing a Set of Leader Qualifications

Long before an application is created or an interview scheduled, supervisors need to know what qualities a good SI leader should possess. The *Supplemental Instruction Supervisor Manual* (University of Missouri – Kansas City, 2004d) lists the following minimum qualifications for an SI leader: (a) sophomore or higher class standing; (b) cumulative GPA of 3.0 or above; (c) content-competency, as determined by the course instructor; and (d) sufficient interpersonal skills, as determined by the SI supervisor. In order to determine what additional qualifications are valuable at a specific institution, supervisors may find it helpful to use a rubric that will lead them through the process of developing a customized set of leader requirements. Kathleen Speed (2005), an SI Supervisor at Texas A&M University, recommends supervisors begin by listing the qualities of a good leader. Typically included in this category are the criteria listed above, but other characteristics may include dependability, an outgoing personality, attention to detail, availability, flexibility, attendance at SI sessions, and even good hygiene.

In general, the characteristics of good leaders seem to fall into three basic categories: (a) social (pertaining to the leader's ability to interact successfully with faculty, students, and SI staff to represent the SI program positively on campus at all times), (b) pedagogical (relating to the leader's knowledge of the content area, desire to maintain the integrity of the SI model by encouraging collaboration among students, ability to resist dominating sessions or relecturing, and willingness to plan sessions using SI strategies), and (c) logistical (referring to the leader's ability to complete required paperwork, adhere to specific directions, attend sessions and meetings, and manage groups successfully). Supervisors will need to prioritize these areas when considering an application and interview process.

In a study conducted at UMKC in 2004, students rated their satisfaction with SI sessions in a specific course. Satisfaction levels were then correlated with their ratings of their leader on many qualities. The relationship between the leaders' social skills and the students' perceptions of helpfulness with the sessions was found to be statistically significant ($p < .05$; Stout & McDaniel, 2004). This finding suggests that the most important area to consider when hiring may be the social skills of the leaders. Many supervisors might rank pedagogical skills as the second most important area followed by logistical skills.

Supervisors need not expect applicants to possess all of the qualities necessary to be a good leader prior to receiving training. Rather, as the third step in this process, Speed (2005) asks supervisors to consider which areas (i.e., social, logistical, or pedagogical) are most teachable. In general, social skills, because they are rooted in cultural practices and formed over many years, may be the most difficult to influence in the limited amount of time available for training. Gaining specific pedagogical and logistical skills during the preterm training is likely achievable for most leaders. In order to help leaders gain these skills, however, supervisors must first know what limitations students already have in these areas. In this regard, the application and interview process can be thought of as placement exams, identifying the level of social and other skills students bring to the program and the kinds of training they are most likely to need.

Getting the Word Out: Recruiting SI Leaders

SI program administrators need to begin hiring for the next semester before the current term is half over. Ideally, many leaders will return for one or more terms, but programs can only reasonably expect to rehire 50% of their leaders. The overall marketing and reputation of the program significantly impacts the ability to attract good SI leaders, perhaps even more than compensation. Returning leaders or mentors (experienced leaders who have been trained to assist supervisors with session observation and supervision) are often the most effective recruiters. They are approachable and relate to other students as peers, making them ideal for representing the program at college information fairs, orientations, and as members of student organizations. Some institutions even have an SI student organization, which helps acquaint students with the SI program and leadership opportunities through social events, guest speakers, and SI attendance drives.

Most institutions offer multiple job opportunities on campus, so representing the SI program as an ideal work environment will aid in recruiting students. If SI leaders maintain a friendly demeanor when visiting lectures and facilitating SI sessions, they promote this image to potential candidates. While programs will want to ensure that financial compensation is on par with other campus employment opportunities, other forms of nonmonetary compensation (e.g., parking passes, independent study credit, merit-based scholarships for returning leaders, or research opportunities) may also be worth investigating.

Many supervisors have found word-of-mouth to be the most productive and cost-effective method of recruitment. SI leaders, because they have worked so closely with the students, are an invaluable source of recommendations and insight about the suitability of specific candidates. One of the best investments a supervisor can make in recruitment for an SI program is to keep the lines of communication open with participating faculty. If faculty enjoy working with the program and appreciate the benefits it provides their students, they will be more likely to take time to recommend students. Other strategies for recruiting students include advertising on campus bulletin boards, in campus newspapers, via e-mail announcements, and cold-calling students who have earned high grades in a targeted course.

Screening Applicants: A Three-Phase Process

The Center for Academic Enhancement at Texas A&M University provides SI leaders for 60 course sections each term and has developed a three-phase application and interview process (Johnson, 2005) to manage their large pool of leader applicants. Although there are not many programs as large as A&M's, their hiring model is designed for efficiency, and all supervisors can benefit from the time it will save. Stage one is completion of an online application form asking students to supply basic information that will be used to verify whether they meet the minimum requirements. It also asks general questions about the applicants' study habits, what SI's they have attended and how often, and what they understand the purpose of SI to be. Many programs currently use a form similar to this one, either online or in hard copy, as their only requirement of applicants. Some also require students to submit an academic transcript. If this is the only required form, once it is determined that the applicant meets the minimum requirements, the supervisor then decides whether or not to interview, often based on the answers the student provided to the general questions about SI and study habits.

In the second phase of the application process developed by Texas A&M's Center for Academic Enhancement, applicants who pass the first step are invited via e-mail to complete a second online form. The second questionnaire asks them to read a peer-reviewed article on SI entitled, "Inside Supplemental Instruction Sessions: One Model of What Happens That Improves Grades and Retention" (Congos & Schoeps, 1998), and write a response to the article. Supervisors then have the opportunity to judge how teachable the student is by comparing his or her answers to the general questions on the first form and his or her response to the peer-reviewed article on SI. An applicant who did not attend SI and did not seem to believe studying in groups provided any benefit to students may not be a poor leader candidate if he or she is able to recognize the value of SI as presented in the scholarly article and reflects this change in the written response.

Finally, the third stage of this process involves interviewing those applicants who meet requirements for open leader positions and have completed the first two phases successfully. Although one interviewer is sufficient, supervisors can invite colleagues or experienced leaders to take part in the interview. The additional set of observations can be invaluable. In order to be as equitable as possible, each interviewee should be asked the same questions. An interviewer can easily be sidetracked depending on the responses from the student, so it is important to keep a list of questions to which he or she can refer throughout the interview. Texas A&M's Center for Academic Enhancement divides the questions into five categories: (a) general questions, (b) instructability, (c) educational philosophy, (d) autonomy/intrinsic motivation, and (e) leadership (see chapter appendix for sample questions). After each group of questions, the interviewer has an area for comments and scoring. Completed during the interview or as soon as possible afterward, scoring can help quantify an applicant's qualifications so that he or she may be more easily compared to other candidates. While it is tempting to hire a good candidate at the interview, supervisors should take some time to discuss the applicant with a co-interviewer, if present, and to compare the applicant to other qualified candidates. If possible, supervisors should offer positions to strong applicants within a few days to avoid giving the impression that the supervisor is not interested and having applicants accept other positions on campus.

Priorities for Preterm Versus Ongoing Training

Often, a one- or two-day, preterm workshop is expected to produce fully educated leaders ready to lead sessions, interact with faculty, and collect accurate data. Unrealistic expectations like these can lead to frustration when leaders still need guidance and practice after the workshop. A more sensible approach is to think of leadership education as an ongoing process. Leaders who attended SI as students will be advanced students at the preterm workshop. After the workshop, all leaders will know the fundamentals of SI but will still need practice planning and facilitating sessions and mastering session strategies. Returning leaders will learn something new each semester they work with the program.

By the end of the preterm training workshop, leaders should feel prepared for the first day of class and their introductory speech. They should understand the philosophical implications of their position as an SI leader: becoming a part of higher education with its purpose of liberation and personal improvement and being an agent of positive change in the lives of students for years to come. They should have a grasp of the more tangible goals of SI as well as understanding the philosophy of learning on which SI is founded; knowing several generic session strategies such as the informal quiz, simple jigsaws, and note review; knowing how to plan flexible sessions; being comfortable meeting with the course instructor; and being prepared to spend 12-15 hours each week attending lectures and planning, facilitating, and debriefing their sessions.

Skills such as dealing with problem students in sessions, using a wide variety of session strategies, and planning effective pre- and postexam review sessions need not be emphasized in the preterm workshop. These can be postponed until the ongoing training meetings and one-on-one planning and debriefing of sessions that will occur throughout the semester. Having clear objectives for the preterm training and helping leaders understand that not everything has to be addressed immediately should give leaders the confidence they need without overwhelming them.

Structuring the Preterm Workshop

The International Center for SI recommends that a preterm training session lasts at least 8 hours or up to 16 hours (i.e., one or two days or a series of evening workshops). More is always better, but finding 16 hours when all leaders are available is difficult. And, although the date should be set far in advance (based on the start date of the semester), some of the best applicants will have conflicting obligations. It is tempting to hire them anyway, but doing so can undermine the entire program, especially on a small campus. Students will know that some leaders are allowed to skip the training, so more applicants will have excuses. In addition, the supervisor will need to make up the training with each leader who missed it, taking valuable time that would be better spent observing SI sessions. Those leaders will have difficulty mastering group facilitation because they were trained one-on-one, without the benefit of collaborative learning. Not only is that an ineffective learning practice, it undermines the foundation of the SI model. Observing sessions and debriefing with leaders allows supervisors to address the learning curve of each leader, but one-on-one training cannot replace the essential, collaborative elements of the preterm training workshop.

Size and Participants

The ideal size for a training workshop is the same as that for an SI session, 5 to 15 students. If the session is larger, dividing the leaders into groups of four or five and, if possible, assigning a returning leader or mentor to each group is a satisfactory accommodation. The experienced SI staff will provide the leaders with additional guidance during small-group work. Some supervisors may choose to mandate that returning leaders repeat the same training each semester, but this is not absolutely necessary. If not required to attend the entire session, they should still be present for a portion of the workshop. This will ensure that you have some returning leaders there the entire time without requiring them to attend both days.

To foster returning leaders' interest in the training workshop, changes should be made to the training agenda each semester. Keeping up with publications in the field, subscribing to the SI-Net e-mail listserv (a resource for connecting with hundreds of SI supervisors by sending a single e-mail; see the UMKC web site for subscription information), attending and presenting at regional, national, and international conferences on SI or teaching and learning practices to exchange new ideas with your colleagues will ensure that supervisors find fresh ideas for each semester. Returning leaders and mentors are often happy to model specific session strategies for new leaders during the workshop. This is helpful for trainees to see because it exposes them to a variety of facilitation techniques, showing them the SI model in many forms, and allowing them to be creative with their own styles. Of course, some leaders will be stronger with some strategies than others, so asking them to prepare a strategy they have used successfully several times is a wise choice.

Team-Building

Although it is often overlooked, team-building is an important part of leader training. Depending on the type and size of institution, leaders may or may not know each other already. Instead of relying on icebreaker activities alone, encouraging leaders to socialize by providing meals or snacks at the workshop, even if the budget is tight, is a more informal approach. Frequent short breaks of 10 minutes or so are almost necessary to keep everyone fresh, and they can be arranged to allow time for leaders to mingle over food and drinks. Assigned seats at the training are a good idea as well. Based on what they know about the leader trainees already, supervisors can group together students who are likely to draw each other out. Seating can be rearranged after the first day of training, if necessary, after the supervisor observes how the students interact. Returning leaders and mentors should be encouraged to be friendly and welcoming to new leaders; this will do much to set the tone for the workshop.

Underlying Pedagogy

SI leaders are peer facilitators of group study sessions. Since they will not be lecturing or delivering content themselves but will be guiding students in the process of learning, they are less like college-level instructors and more like secondary education teachers. Lecturing them on their duties, recommended strategies, and expected performance, therefore, will not prepare them for their dynamic role as a facilitator. Instead, supervisors are encouraged to look to teacher education and use modeling, guided practice, and independent practice (Hunter, 1990) to prepare leaders for the sophisticated tasks of modeling and guiding effective student learning. Hunter's Elements of Lesson Design is a widely known model for preparing lesson plans presented to preservice teachers. Table 1 translates Hunter's terms into those used in the SI community.

Table 1

Elements of an SI Leaders' Training

Lesson-planning element	SI term	Explanation
Anticipatory set	Advanced organizer	Focuses students on task at hand; reviews and corrects previously learned information
Objective	Set agenda	Tells students what they will be doing that day
Input	Course materials	Gives students information from text, films, teacher, observation, or the Internet
Modeling	Modeling	Shows students tasks they will shortly have to perform; encourages input and evaluation from students
Checking for understanding	Checking for understanding	Asks students to apply what they have learned to determine whether they understand
Guided or monitored practice	Session strategy	Allows students to practice what they have learned
Independent practice	No specific SI term. Students are asked to practice independently during portions of strategies such as the informal quiz and one-minute paper. Leaders practice independently when they lead their own sessions throughout the semester.	Asks students individually to complete an assignment using the skills they have learned (homework)

Source: Adapted from Hunter (1990, p. 79).

Preparation

Supervisors can expect to spend 5 to10 hours preparing for the preterm leader training workshop. This includes time spent gathering resources, setting an agenda, selecting lecture tapes or scheduling guest speakers (to provide content for mock SI sessions), planning for strategies to be modeled by the supervisor, assigning strategies to be modeled by returning leaders or mentors, preparing a presentation on the history of SI, making copies of all handouts and manuals, ordering food, and booking a venue. Smaller programs may be able to use the SI office for the workshop, but larger programs may need to schedule additional facilities in order to be able to seat participants in small groups without overcrowding.

Once the preterm workshop is scheduled, supervisors can find helpful resources provided by the University of Missouri – Kansas City (UMKC). As the home of he International Center for SI, UMKC is the only source of many copyrighted materials such as the *Learning to Train SI Leaders: A Manual for SI Supervisors* (University of Missouri – Kansas City, 2004a), *Supplemental Instruction Leader's Guide* (University of Missouri – Kansas City, 2004b), *Supplemental Instruction Leader Resource Manual* (University of Missouri – Kansas City, 2004c), and the *Supplemental Instruction Supervisor Manual* (University of Missouri – Kansas City, 2004d). While this chapter highlights information included in the training manual, it is impossible to include all of the detail and useful forms that make it up.

As it is difficult to accurately describe the informal yet productive, planned yet flexible atmosphere of an SI session or the hands-off approach of some of the best leaders, demonstration sessions are an important part of SI leader training. The demonstration sessions show leaders what an ideal session will look like. UMKC has produced taped lectures by some of their best faculty and live, unscripted SI sessions in several disciplines that campuses can use as part of their training. Supervisors may choose to use the taped lectures as content on which to base simulated sessions. Guest speakers are also a good option for this portion of the training; a lively lecture can reinvigorate participants, especially near the end of the workshop. The demonstration sessions typically are used to show leaders what an ideal session will look like.

Teaching Leaders Good Pedagogical Practices

Modeling

Many students arrive at college having had bad group work experiences in high school. Assigning small groups to work on tasks that are not designed to hold each member accountable or that pit members against each other often result in negative feelings because one or two people end up doing all the work. Successful collaborative learning must be carefully planned and facilitated, and if SI supervisors do not model good facilitator behavior in the sessions they conduct—the preterm and ongoing trainings—leaders who are already skeptical will become relecturers or homework tutors in their own sessions. In short, supervisors cannot employ the maxim, "Do as I say, not as I do," and resort to lecturing or passive learning strategies to teach leaders how to facilitate SI sessions.

Before the workshop. Modeling good facilitator behavior begins before workshop participants even arrive. Just as supervisors ask leaders to do for their sessions, supervisors should also plan the workshop carefully. The agenda will already be set, and all tasks that will be assigned to participants to complete over specific content (as part of learning strategy modeling) should be completed prior to the workshop. For example, if the supervisor will be asking leaders to view a taped lecture and then form a matrix of the material, the supervisor should already have completed the matrix. This will bring to light any potential problems with the design of the activity and allow the supervisor to adjust his or her plan, if necessary.

The room should be arranged so that participants are divided into groups of no more than five students. This will allow the supervisor to arrange seating by placing nametags at each chair, and it will help to foster collaboration among the leaders. Food should be set out, and manuals should be distributed. Any video tapes to be used should be queued to the appropriate start point. The supervisor should bring pencils or pens for leaders to use since they may forget them.

Trainer behaviors. Supervisors and returning leaders or mentors should lead the training workshop as though they were leading an SI session. The facilitator of each activity should sit down with the group whenever possible, in order to avoid being the focal point and to encourage students to address each other. While facilitating, trainers should use at least three seconds of Wait-Time 1 (i.e., the time that elapses between asking a question and repeating, rephrasing, or asking another question) and Wait-Time 2 (i.e., the time that elapses between a student response and the next utterance) to allow participants the opportunity to formulate answers and build on each other's responses. This will encourage participation from the group. Facilitators should redirect questions whenever appropriate, using verbal and nonverbal methods. When it is helpful to draw a diagram or note important points from the conversation on the board, the facilitator should ask for a volunteer from the group to take notes. These simple methods will demonstrate to leaders that the supervisor does in practice what he or she also imparts in theory.

Demonstration session tapes. Tapes of live, unscripted demonstration sessions allow some of the best and most experienced leaders to model a real SI session for new leaders. Watching an ideal session on tape will help leader trainees understand exactly what supervisors are asking them to do. New leaders will often view an example of an ideal session and find it lacking in structure or formality. Usually, it is because experienced leaders "train" their students to rely on each other as they work through material, referring to the leader only for clarification as needed. This is an important reaction to note and discuss in the workshop, and supervisors should be sure to debrief the tape so that similar observations and questions can surface.

Guided Practice: The Planning Rubric

As educators, we know that a successful, collaborative classroom experience necessitates significant planning, but new leaders often underestimate the time it requires. Many a supervisor has observed a leader flounder in a session, only to discover that his or her plan—to answer questions or "go over" material—was woefully inadequate. For this reason, planning is emphasized in the preterm workshop.

In order to prepare leaders to practice planning, supervisors must structure the workshop so that, by the time the leaders are asked to create a session plan, the trainers have facilitated and debriefed two or three suitable session strategies. Because many SI programs are made up of leaders in a variety of disciplines (e.g., history, accounting, biology, chemistry, philosophy, and nursing) trainers usually model generic strategies such as note review, the informal quiz, matrices, board work models, and vocabulary development (see Appendix A at the end of this monograph for a glossary of common strategies or the *Supplemental Instruction Resource Manual* for more detailed information). After each lecture tape or guest speaker presents content for a mock session, the participants work together to plan a session, following the planning rubric (see chapter appendix for examples). The leaders follow each step of the rubric to assure that all reasonable contingencies are considered and to establish good planning habits for the future. Supervisors should instruct them to choose from only those strategies that have already been modeled as they plan.

After a specified amount of time, the small groups or pairs share their plans with the large group. As they share their session plans, the other participants and trainers will have an opportunity to guide and correct them. Most new leaders will make the same planning mistakes: wanting to cover all material, not only the most difficult; underestimating how much time students will need to practice and master the content; failing to plan a session strategy, expecting students to just answer questions or quiz others with no structure; and not anticipating that students might attend without their books or notes. At this point, the supervisor should ask everyone to pick the two best plans. Once everyone agrees that there is at least one good plan, a leader trainee should be solicited to lead the group in a simulated session based on that plan. After the training workshop, all leaders should be required to plan at least their first three sessions with a supervisor, using the rubric.

Independent Practice: Session Simulations

Although most college-level instruction is based on lecture, those who teach processes such as classroom facilitation turn to case studies, simulations, and even drama to help teachers prepare for the real thing (Coppens, 2002; Hoelscher, 1996; Mandinach & Cline, 1994; McCann, 2003). Similarly, leaders benefit substantially from session simulations during preterm training because they have the opportunity to make and correct mistakes before their first real session.

In general, three 20-minute simulations should be included in a two-day, 16-hour training session and at least one simulation in shorter sessions. The content from taped lectures or guest speakers (no more than 20 minutes) used to develop session rubrics will also provide material for the simulated session(s). It is important to choose material that will be challenging for the leaders (e.g., advanced calculus or organic chemistry). SI works because students who attend are motivated by a specific goal: getting a better grade in the class. In order for the mock session to simulate the activity and atmosphere of a real SI session as closely as possible, the leaders-in-training must also be challenged to learn the material. If the lecture material is review for them, the simulation will be artificial.

In general, it is best to schedule the session simulation to begin after a short break. This will give the trainee who volunteered to lead the session an opportunity to prepare by talking with the supervisor and reviewing the plan identified by other participants as the strongest. During the session simulation, leaders should be reminded to do everything they would do in a real session: arrange the seats in a circle, pass around the participation log, set the agenda, redirect questions, use wait-time, and encourage students to help each other. Of course, a new leader will not lead a perfect session the first time. If possible, select a mentor to observe the session and debrief with the leader in front of the group. Then audience members (new and returning leaders) can comment on what they saw. For the first simulation, debriefing the finer points of facilitation like use of wait time or question redirection may be premature, but by the third mock session, the volunteer leader will have benefited from seeing the general structure of two simulations, and the supervisor can usually address the details of facilitation without overwhelming him or her. At all times, however, the attitude of the debriefing should remain one of constructive criticism, not negativity.

Other Topics to Address in Preterm Training

Many supervisors focus, in preterm training, on the pedagogical aspects of an SI leader's position. This is understandable since the facilitation of successful sessions is a sophisticated skill to master, but the administrative and ambassadorial duties that SI leaders assume are equally important.

Data Collection

Participation logs are sign-in sheets that are used to track student participation (see chapter appendix). Leaders are responsible for sending one around at every SI session. At the end of the term, the logs are compared to the course roster in order to determine which students comprised the "SI group" versus the "non-SI group." Thus, the participation logs are essential for program assessment. One of the most effective ways to impress upon leaders how crucial those participation logs are is to show some data charts that demonstrate the effectiveness of SI. Newer programs with limited assessment data can obtain sample charts demonstrating the effectiveness of SI on a variety of subjects and at all different types of institutions from the International Center for SI at UMKC. After showing these to leaders, perhaps in a PowerPoint presentation, supervisors can explain to leaders that without their care in collecting accurate, legible records of attendance at each and every session (and accurate entry of that data into a database, if applicable), these data would not be collected or interpreted. Further, the supervisor can explain the vital connection between assessment data and program funding. This approach usually convinces most leaders that while what actually happens in the session is their primary responsibility, records of those sessions are essential to the continuation of the program.

Ambassadorial Duties

SI leaders are the most visible part of an SI program. One of the primary purposes of attending the course lecture is to remain a visible source of support for students. For this reason, leaders must be reminded that they are representatives of the program at all times they are on campus, even when they are not acting in an SI capacity. Students often admire SI leaders, so they will pay attention to their behavior. Instructors respect leaders as accomplished, motivated students, and so they, too, observe leaders carefully. Supervisors should encourage leaders to act as model students in each of their courses, not just the course targeted by SI. Leaders should be respectful of campus rules, be courteous and polite to campus staff and students, and act with integrity at all times. Modeling is an important approach to communicating this to leaders; supervisors should observe the same guidelines when they are on campus. Preparing a list of SI leader etiquette that is particular to the institution is helpful and should be distributed at the preterm workshop.

Supervisors should also allow some time in the training workshop to discuss the nuances of the leaders' role on campus. As with other aspects of the training, hands-on activities provide better learning opportunities for students than straight lecture. The *Supplemental Instruction Leader's Guide* (University of Missouri – Kansas City, 2004a, p. 20-21) presents several scenarios that leaders may encounter throughout the semester. These include an instructor asking the leader to lecture in his or her absence, a student sharing a serious personal problem with the leader, and a student asking a leader for his or her notes. Discussion of how leaders should handle these situations will elucidate the leaders' role and their relationship to students and instructors. It is helpful to spend a few minutes discussing them in small groups and then sharing each answer with the large group.

Finally, leaders should spend time at the preterm workshop preparing to introduce SI to the students on the first day of classes. Some programs may have visual aids that leaders can use in class, such as brochures, PowerPoint presentations, or promotional videos. At that point, the main goal is to get students to come to SI. Leaders should limit speeches to the basics, answering the following questions for students: What is SI? What is in it for me? Where or when do I go? What will I do when I am there? What are the leader's qualifications? Where can I find him or her? Supervisors can help leaders by having them practice this introduction in front of the group during the training.

Observing and Debriefing Sessions: A One-on-One Training Opportunity

Session observations often fall into the category of performance review. As such, they may occur only once or twice a semester, but weekly or biweekly observations and prompt debriefs offer an opportunity for ongoing, customized leader (and mentor) training. In addition, time spent observing and debriefing with leaders is an investment in the quality of the SI experience for students and can significantly reduce the amount of time spent recruiting leaders each semester. That is because students who attend ideal SI sessions are benefiting from the study time, seeing an improvement in their grades, and becoming supporters of SI. These students do not attend SI expecting a quick fix or answers to homework assignments. Instead, they expect that their leader will have planned a discipline-appropriate, collaborative strategy by which they can attack the subject matter as a group. And that is what they will expect from each SI session they attend, including the ones they lead themselves in the subsequent semesters.

Skills such as redirecting questions, using wait-time, and managing session time wisely can be introduced, explained, and practiced in the preterm workshop, but the group likely will not master these skills until they lead their own sessions. Revisiting them during the ongoing training meetings is wise. It is through on-the-job training, however, as a student meets his or her own academic obligations and those of being a model student and SI leader, that his or her ability to achieve a productive balance improves. Mentors, experienced leaders, and SI supervisors must guide new leaders in the formation of these skills by observing them regularly and offering structured, specific feedback. (Two versions of SI session observation forms are included in the chapter appendix.)

Guidelines

Because poor planning is the primary cause of unproductive sessions, the *Leader Resource Manual* (University of Missouri – Kansas City, 2004c) dedicates 55 pages to planning and session strategies. Requiring SI leaders to plan their first three sessions in the SI office and have them approved by a mentor or supervisor can prevent many facilitation problems. The students' expectations are set early, so leaders need to begin planning collaborative activities, redirecting questions, and using wait-time immediately. Even if only a short chat is possible right away, supervisors should talk over observations with the leader immediately after the session, especially those early in the semester. Productive debriefings always begin with the supervisor asking the leaders how they thought the session went, soliciting their view of the session before making any comments. Supervisors predominantly practice positive reinforcement and limit their constructive suggestions, targeting only one or two areas for improvement at a given time. The leader and supervisor then work together to arrive at specific tactics that will improve the sessions. Depending on the problem, solutions will vary. In general, feedback for new leaders will focus on arranging the room in a circle, redirecting questions, using wait-time, tweaking facilitation of certain techniques, and time management.

Ongoing Training Sessions

Without a formal opportunity to reflect on their practices, teachers often teach how they were taught, and SI leaders often lead how they were led. After the fundamentals of SI are addressed in the preterm training, leaders still need a setting in which they may share their experiences, practice new strategies, and polish their facilitation skills. Most SI programs include some amount of ongoing training, offering support to leaders throughout the semester. These meetings are especially important when the preterm training is less than 16 hours.

Purpose and Frequency

Scheduling ongoing training meetings accomplishes several goals: (a) reinvigorating sessions by introducing leaders to new session strategies, sharing new discoveries in pedagogy or learner-centered research, and expanding on topics introduced in the preterm workshop; (b) addressing practical concerns such as scheduling exam reviews, managing large sessions, handling dominant or disruptive students, and finding enough time to fulfill all of their obligations; (c) providing guidance in planning special sessions such as exam reviews or postexam reviews; (d) providing experienced leaders and mentors with an opportunity to research and present topics; and (e) simply gathering leaders together several times each semester to share their experiences and support each other. Planning a one-hour training every other week should be manageable for both supervisors and leaders. For large programs, supervisors may need to schedule two different meeting times and present the same content or practice the same strategy at both times so that all leaders can participate.

When deciding what to address in your meetings, continue to involve returning leaders and mentors in the training process. Supervisors can give them some autonomy in the process by providing them with a list of possible topics and asking a leader or pair of leaders to choose one to prepare for a meeting. They may need assistance locating sources, but most leaders would rather do the research and planning required to lead the meeting than sit through the same topic twice.

Suggested Topics

Ongoing training meetings should provide leaders with tools and information that go beyond the basics of SI. While supervisors should model generic session strategies at the preterm workshop, ongoing trainings are an opportunity to help leaders master more sophisticated strategies such as advanced organizers, reciprocal questioning, and those that use writing in SI sessions. Leaders will also benefit from presentations of research in the field of teaching and learning or even psychology or communication. Any information that can be applied while facilitating an SI session can be helpful.

Leaders also appreciate a thoughtful progression in ongoing training meeting topics, so the meetings should correspond to what the leaders are doing throughout the term. There will be points in the semester when leaders will be more interested in practical topics they can apply immediately such as planning exam review sessions, managing disruptive students, and polishing facilitation skills. Later in the semester, when leaders have only a few sessions left and may not be able to introduce new strategies to the students (but will be returning for future semesters), it is best to focus on theoretical or research-based topics that prompt discussion and influence pedagogy indirectly.

Conclusion

Recruiting and training leaders and mentors can be the most demanding part of being an SI supervisor. Each semester, we face the challenge of staffing our programs with qualified, personable leaders. From the application process to the ongoing training meetings, supervisors can ease this perennial burden by approaching it in a systematic manner. This chapter has presented supervisors with (a) suggestions for establishing criteria for good SI leader candidates; (b) proven methods of recruiting, screening, and interviewing applicants; (c) tips on prioritizing training goals; (d) structure for a preterm training workshop; (e) guidelines for teaching leaders good pedagogy through modeling, guided practice, and independent practice; and (f) ideas for continuing the training process through ongoing meetings and session observation and debriefing.

Few positions open to undergraduate students require completion of such a rigorous training program without also providing course credit. Creating a credit-bearing course for SI leaders would provide them with the recognition they deserve for the learning process they undergo as they progress throughout the semester. With the addition of readings in learning theory, application of theory to practice, and reflective and analytic writings, the SI leader training program would merit academic acknowledgement. Supervisors interested in developing a credit-bearing course as the future of leader training, however, should research possible departments on their campus in which to house such a program. As field practitioners, we are also the pioneers; it is our responsibility to hold our leaders to high standards and also to raise those standards as they exceed them.

References

Congos, D., & Schoeps, N. (1998). Inside Supplemental Instruction sessions: One model of what happens that improves grades and retention. *Research and Teaching in Developmental Education, 15*(1), 47-62.

Coppens, H. (2002). Training teachers' behaviour. *Research in Drama Education, 7*(2), 195-206.

Hoelscher, K. (1996). Using simulations to develop cultural sensitivity in preservice teachers: The Heelotia experience. *Multicultural Education, 3*(3), 39-43.

Hunter, M. (1990). Lesson design helps achieve the goals of science instruction. *Educational Leadership, 48*(4), 79-81.

Johnson, R. (2005, May). *From hiring to reporting statistics and everything in-between: Here's how Texas A&M University does it.* Conference session presented at the Regional Conference on SI, College Station, TX.

Mandinach, E. B., & Cline, H. F. (1994). Modeling and simulation in the secondary school curriculum: The impact on teachers. *Interactive Learning Environments, 4*(3), 271-289.

McCann, T. M. (2003). Imagine this: Using scenarios to promote authentic discussion. *English Journal, 92*(6), 31-39.

Speed, K. (2005, May). *Hiring and misfiring: Am I getting what I want?* Conference session presented at a Regional Conference on SI, College Station, TX.

Stout, L., & McDaniel, A. (2004). [Factors influencing students' perceptions of helpfulness of Supplemental Instruction]. Unpublished raw data.

University of Missouri – Kansas City. (2004a). *Learning to train SI Leaders: A manual for SI supervisors.* Kansas City, MO: The Curators of the University of Missouri.

University of Missouri – Kansas City. (2004b). *Supplemental Instruction leader's guide.* Kansas City, MO: The Curators of the University of Missouri.

University of Missouri – Kansas City. (2004c). *Supplemental Instruction leader resource manual.* Kansas City, MO: The Curators of the University of Missouri.

University of Missouri – Kansas City. (2004d). *Supplemental Instruction supervisor manual.* Kansas City, MO: The Curators of the University of Missouri.

Appendix

Sample Interview Questions for SI Leader Applicants[1]

General

1. Why do you want to be an SI leader?
2. What are your impressions of SI?
   a. What do you think SI is designed to accomplish?
   b. Have you ever attended an SI session?
      i. Did the leader follow the SI model?
      ii. What would you do differently?
3. As an SI leader, you must be prepared for various situations that will test your patience and ability to remain cordial regardless of the circumstances. Can you describe a situation in which your patience and your ability to remain in control have been tested?

Instructability

1. What have been/are some of your frustrations with/during your college experience?
   a. How have you resolved/attempted to resolve these?
2. How comfortable would you be with sharing/presenting study skills to peers?

Educational Philosophy

1. In your view, what is the difference between teaching and facilitating?
2. When you see others struggling academically, how do you
   a. overcome that?
   b. convince them to apply the things that work for you?
3. Scenario: Ill-prepared students come to your SI sessions and consistently pressure you to relecture the material. How do you address this?

Autonomy/Intrinsic Motivation

1. How do you motivate yourself?
2. Describe how you have handled shifting priorities and juggling schedules in the past in order to get several things accomplished (e.g., studies, extracurricular commitments).
3. What do you think are the biggest challenges for SI leaders?

Leadership

1. Describe the most effective team of which you have been a part.
   a. What made it effective?
   b. What role did you play?

2. Describe an instance when you were in a leadership role and the people whom you were leading were of the same age as you.
   a. How did you view yourself? (e.g., equal partner, authoritarian leader)
   b. How did you handle "disciplinary" problems?
   c. How did you motivate your peers?
3. Briefly discuss how you would deal with a regular attendee who is consistently behind the rest of the attendees.

---

[1] Copyright © 2006, Center for Academic Enhancement, Texas A&M University. All rights reserved. Used with permission.

Participation Log

SI Leader: _____ **Course #:** _____ **Date:** _____

Day of Week: _____ **Time Began:** _____ **Time Ended:** _____

Is this the last session before an exam? Y   N   **If so, Exam #:** _____

PLEASE PRINT CLEARLY

1. _____   12. _____

2. _____   13. _____

3. _____   14. _____

4. _____   15. _____

5. _____   16. _____

6. _____   17. _____

7. _____   18. _____

8. _____   19. _____

9. _____   20. _____

10. _____   21. _____

11. _____   22. _____

SI Observation Record A

Observer:_____   **SI Leader:** _____

Date: _____   **Course:** _____

Number Attending:_____

Qualities	Satisfactory	Need for Improvement
Room arranged for group work (circle or semi-circle).		
Session begins on time.		
Participation Logs filled in.		
SI leader prepared.		
Planning the SI Session sheet available.		
Agenda set at beginning of session.		
Advanced Organizer used.		
Students doing most of the talking (helping each other).		
Effective use of questions (open-ended, higher-level).		
Leader uses appropriate wait time.		
Appropriate processing activities used.		
If available, were the worksheets helpful?		
Students referring to textbooks and notes.		
Leader involves all students.		
Leader addresses students' needs and questions.		
Leader is knowledgeable of content material.		
Leader sets appropriate tone for session.		
Time managed efficiently during session.		
Summary and closure.		
Students seemed to gain understanding.		

Additional Comments:

SI Observation Record B

Activities	Observer's Comments
Introduction to SI session Participation Log Materials used by SI leader Activities in the session, Evaluation used (e.g., quiz, oral recall) Closure of session	

Chapter 6

Strategies for Adapting Supplemental Instruction to Specific Academic Disciplines

Sandra Zerger

Supplemental Instruction (SI) began with some reflection about the nature of study skills and learning and how students perceive their need for strategic guidance. Deanna Martin, founder of SI, was concerned that students would have little interest in stand-alone study strategies courses or would be unable to transfer acquired skills to other courses. In addition, she observed that students often attributed their lack of success in courses to external factors, such as a particular course topic or a certain professor, rather than to their own challenges in knowing *how* to learn. SI was conceptualized with these concerns in mind—to incorporate study strategies within a contextual framework, with clear demonstration of how such skills could be used, and to offer such support to *all* students, regardless of actual or perceived ability, in courses that were known to be difficult. Thus, in the ensuing decades since its establishment, SI has developed or adapted numerous strategies to support students in demanding courses. Some of these include the informal quiz (University of Missouri – Kansas City, 2004), note review (University of Missouri – Kansas City), reciprocal questioning (Manzo, 1969), matrices (de Jong & Ferguson-Hessler, 1996), and vocabulary development (Bower, Clark, Lesgold, & Winzenz, 1969; Spiegel & Barufaldi, 1994). These strategies have proven to be valuable for courses across a wide variety of disciplines. (For descriptions of strategies discussed throughout the chapter, please check the *Glossary of Terms* at the end of this monograph.)

In order to prepare all leaders regardless of the subject area they will be supporting, SI training usually focuses on general strategies that are transferable, and, historically, the program has relied on supervisors and leaders to adapt these techniques to specific content. However, increasingly, supervisors and leaders are requesting strategies more specific to individual disciplines. Consequently, the topic of adapting SI strategies to specific disciplines will be explored in this chapter.

Ontology, Epistemology, and Methodology Differ by Discipline

During the 1980s, the theory and practice of psychologists studying learning shifted from a purely cognitive emphasis to one that focused on the social dimensions of learning. Educators, including those in SI, became increasingly aware of the value of collaborative learning and, at the same time, began to value the extent to which students were indoctrinated into the culture of their respective disciplines (Ackerman, 1991; Geisler, 1994a, 1994b). Social scientists began to appreciate not only the differences in subject matter that influence various learning styles across the disciplines, but also the impact of the diverse characteristics of the communities themselves. As educators, we identify general strategies that can guide the conscious aspects of thinking and recognize that thinking is a highly contextualized activity manifested in different ways in different contexts. We have discovered that some learning strategies are generic and transferable across disciplines, while others are specific to certain bodies of knowledge. The key to "expertise . . . becomes a *knowing that* linked to a *knowing how*" (Geisler, 1994b, p. 44).

All disciplines have conventions—in the ways they structure writing, cite references, and use language—that can vary widely from one discipline to the next (Linton, Madigan, & Johnson, 1994). In one of the earliest articles on discipline-specific writing strategies, Bazerman (1981) analyzed the professional literature in three disciplines: biology, sociology, and literary criticism. He evaluated the extent to which the articles were discipline-specific, as determined by the specificity of the nature of knowledge in terms of the phenomena or topics discussed, the nature of prior knowledge, and the nature of a shared audience perspective. In biology, Bazerman found that the phenomena discussed were well-established (e.g., the location of a certain protein in DNA). Also, prior knowledge was codified, so the author did not need to spend time clarifying and describing what had become foundational knowledge for the essay. For the sociologist, he found that the phenomena must be first established, as the prior literature was often unsettled and open to interpretation; and the audience shared no uniform framework. In literary criticism, Bazerman discovered that the phenomena (e.g., poems) are known, but the object is to recreate subjective poetic moments. The criticism of a poem is particular, while codification is entirely personal, and the literary audience is concerned with private experience.

A plethora of scholarship followed on other indicators of discipline specificity, such as expectations (Herrington, 1985a, 1985b; Walvoord & McCarthy, 1990); social aspects (Devitt, 1991; Wilkins, 1990); use of evidence (Herrington, 1985a); and claims made (Bazerman, 1981, Durst, 1994). Soon, educators and scholars studied the tacit expectations for their own disciplines (see Baum-Brunner, 1997; Coppola & Daniels, 1996; Driskill, Lewis, Stearns & Volz, 1998; Durst, 1994; Glynn, Yeany, & Britton, 1991; Hynd, 1999; Jamison, 2000; Shahn & Costello, 2000; Stockton, 1994). These studies proved fruitful for the adaptation and development of SI strategies.

Generic or Transferable Skills Versus Specific Skills

Since the beginning of SI more than 35 years ago, we have increased our knowledge of how students learn. Much of the research comes from interdisciplinary fields, such as composition theory (discipline-specific literacy or writing across the disciplines), disciplinary pedagogy (especially in physics, chemistry, and biology), and teaching and learning scholarship (e.g., the International Society for Exploring Teaching and Learning or ISETL). When SI was initiated, the prevailing metaphor for teaching was that of the professor pouring knowledge through a funnel directly into students' minds. The modes of presentation were lecture and lab (science), or lecture and discussion groups (social sciences). Content was presented by experts in a rather mechanistic manner. In the 1950s and 1960s, a widely held view among cognitive psychologists was that becoming an expert involved mastering general, transferable strategies, such as keeping a list of learning goals, monitoring actions toward goals, and following prescribed problem-solving rules (Kaufer & Young, 1993).

The model of expertise that assumed general, transferable strategies lessened in the 1970s, as instructors became increasingly concerned with students' ability to learn. Rather, instructors encouraged students to become more active learners, to break out of the passive mode of merely being recipients of knowledge. Research on learning moved away from a focus on general strategies and began to explore more complex models of learning. Studies of mastery, in areas such as chess, began to suggest that experts rely more on recognizing patterns and whole games than on applying general strategies (Chase & Simon, 1973; Chi, Feltovich, & Glaser, 1981; Chi, Glaser, & Rees, 1982). Studies of differences between experts and novices in computer science demonstrated that students working on computers programmed with knowledge in a single subject outperformed students using computers programmed with only general strategies (Kaufer & Young, 1993). Such studies suggested that expertise in one area did not always transfer to other areas. In fact, according to Kaufer and Young, "Expertise relies on a complex model and unspecified interaction between knowledge and general strategies, but experts do benefit from general strategies when they enter unfamiliar areas" (p. 94). Eventually, instructors began talking about the fact that they were not teaching in a vacuum. ·

Tailoring SI Strategies to the Disciplines

Humanities and History

In the humanities and in history, the text or artifact is the object of study. Students often think that history is a collection of dates, names, and events, but historians think it is "a theory-based means of understanding the past and of connecting the past with the present and the future" (Durst, 1994, p. 84). This understanding often requires the historian to show a cause-and-effect relationship. As such, students need to learn how to read and understand texts. When historians read texts, they comprehend not only the literal text, but the subtexts as well—texts of the author's intent, purposes, and goals (Wineburg, 1991). Students read history not as a process of trying to understand the authors' intentions or incorporating the texts into their worldviews, but as gathering information without engaging in the texts themselves (Wineburg). To help students understand historical texts, Hynd (1999) has argued that students should be given multiple accounts of the same event from different authors. The SI session can provide an opportunity for students to understand the background, discuss historians' use of context, cultural biases, events, and types of sources used. The sessions can offer extended discussion, guided reading, including divide-and-conquer activities (i.e., students work in small groups on portions of material and then gather to share results) (University of Missouri – Kansas City, 2004), or debates with groups taking on the viewpoints of the various texts. Students in SI sessions can also practice short writings imitating the rhetorical style of historians.

Other strategies to help students understand history might include an archeological hunt to examine evidence; construction of a matrix, allowing students to write subarguments for each cell of the matrix; or the development of timelines, especially double or triple timelines (with events from multiple places) that provide useful ways to point out cause-and-effect relationships and can aid in organizing information, even if dates are not stressed by the professor.

Natural Sciences

Since much of science is highly structured and codified with general agreement among the scientific community, the task for students is to learn the structure or code. Writing, for example, is not seen as an epistemic activity involving invention, exploration, and organization of ideas, as it is in English, but rather, as a presentation of prior thinking and design and execution of an experiment (Kaufer & Young, 1993). Lab reports, for example, must follow strict conventions because they may be evidence in patent applications and product litigations. So, student notebooks must be string-bound, paginated before written on, written in pen, and lines drawn through unused spaces (Kaufer & Young). SI sessions may be devoted to helping students understand the conventions and characteristics of good lab reports.

Effective textbook use. Science textbooks also are highly structured. Many professors admit that they did not really know a subject thoroughly until they prepared to teach from them. SI sessions should include strategies that engage students in the processes faculty go through to plan their courses. Shahn and Costello (2000) suggest that since faculty, when preparing a lecture, think carefully about what they will say about each main point, students should be asked to do the same in written form, allowing them more opportunity for reflection and revision than possible with oral delivery. Students who think carefully about the structure of the selected texts and course schedule will have a better understanding of how the instructor, an expert, thinks about the material.

Writing exercises. In an instance when an instructor asked an SI leader what would be coming next in the course and why, the leader replied, "Because it is the next chapter." The leader obviously did not think about the how, or the why, of the course structure. The leader's answer typifies an attitude of rote learning or memorization of isolated facts, and thinking that science gives "true" answers, even when the use of explanations and descriptions are requested. What should happen in SI is a way to bring together data to draw conclusions—whether in a lab report, a series of items from the text, or selection of correct multiple-choice answers on an examination. The difference between a C or D grade and an A is often due to the amount of contemplation a subject is given. According to Shahn and Costello (2000), "Poor results offer platitudes reflecting the value of science, while good ones show a considerable degree of reflection" (p. 64).

Writing exercises are important strategies that can be used to help process the often challenging content found in the scientific disciplines. Even if little formal writing is required in a course, writing can serve as a valuable aid to learning and should be incorporated into SI sessions. For example, students can work together to locate an example of a certain type of reaction in a professional journal and write a quiz question from it that is appropriate for the level of the class, including a short statement contextualizing the reaction, a copy of the pages of the journal where the reaction was found, and a citation. The groups then take turns sharing their findings with the large group, and subsequent discussion addresses the following issues: (a) Does the reaction meet the criteria set? (b) Is the question at the level of the class, not above or below? (c) Is the citation correct? (Coppola & Daniels, 1996). Students can also write or orally argue issues from the course, review and refine exam or homework questions, and write one-minute papers to formulate ideas before a discussion or to summarize a session.

In the sciences, students are often given myriad concepts to digest. Many of these concepts are very difficult for students to grasp because they are often counterintuitive to the students' common knowledge. In order to learn and retain the vast amount of material presented—often in very compact form—students need ways to sort and group information. An interesting collaborative laboratory exercise that Coppola and Daniels (1996) call "Who Has the Same Thing as I Do?" easily adapts to SI sessions. Students are given cards with various concepts written on them (e.g., melting point or infrared spectrum). Other cards might have names of substances or theories. Groups or dyads try to match related concepts by discussing how and why they believe the concepts are related. Similar cards could be used to group elements on the periodic chart and learn symbols for the elements. Here the emphasis should be on discovering relationships among the elements—reflected in the periodic chart.

Another strategy for grouping and connecting difficult conceptual material is cognitive mapping. Cognitive mapping allows students to learn connections, understand processes, and learn the vocabulary of the course (Glynn et al., 1991; Robertson, 1990). This technique of diagramming related concepts allows students to visually understand the connections between ideas. The SI leader can demonstrate this strategy for students and, then, as the semester progresses, students can draw their own maps without the leader's assistance. This process is especially dynamic if done in small groups, with each group reporting back to the participants for comparison. Concept maps are just one example of graphic organizers, which have been shown to aid recall and retention of scientific knowledge (Spiegel & Barufaldi, 1994). Drawings, pictures, and slides with material deleted also are useful, as is reorganizing linear text (like lists from a textbook) into spatial representations. All of these strategies can aid in learning and retention (Meltzer, 2005).

Many students mistakenly think that superficial mathematical manipulations will provide the key to success in their science courses. However, students who rely on memorized algorithms to solve problems often have trouble transferring this "learning" to other problems and seldom understand the underlying concepts (Redish & Steinberg, 1999; Robertson, 1990). In SI, therefore, we need to include more than a series of problems for students to solve. We also need to help students sort problems, analyze categories, and look for problems with surface similarities. (See useful information in Driskill et al., 1998). Matrices and vocabulary development strategies—lists of terms at different levels of specificity that students work in pairs to group in meaningful ways and then justify their organization to the other students—are also useful for these purposes.

Mathematics and Engineering

In some respects, mathematics and engineering courses resemble natural science courses, in that they have mathematical problems, and they call on students to be able to formulate answers related to real-life situations. In other respects, mathematics and engineering courses act like language courses, in that a meaningful connection of mathematical symbols represents a type of sentence. Using common language can be a major pedagogical tool for understanding mathematics and applied mathematics (such as engineering). In making the case for the use of a precise language for learning mathematics, Jamison (2000) has argued that, "Once students understand *how* things are said, they can better understand *what* is being said, and only then do they have a chance to know *why* it is said" (p. 45). Yet, many students see mathematics as far removed from language and more as a "collection of arcane rules for manipulating bizarre symbols" (Jamison, p. 45). A great deal of attention has focused on the teaching of mathematics in other nations where students score higher on standardized tests than students in the US (Gonzales et al., 2000; Hoff, 1997; 2001). Many argue that the problem of understanding mathematics results from an overemphasis on teaching procedural techniques for working problems rather than understanding the concepts underlying them (Spiegel & Barufaldi, 1994). The equations and mathematical formulae should be viewed as vehicles for thoughts expressed in mathematical terms. As such, students need help in understanding interrelationships among more sophisticated concepts (Jamison). Too often, SI sessions in mathematics become drill sessions. When that is the case, the efficacy of SI decreases.

The language of math. The codified mode of presentation for mathematics (which has been around since Euclid ca. 300 BC) is definition-theorem-proof (Jamison, 2000). The language of mathematics differs from ordinary language in that it has no time, is devoid of emotion, and is precise. If the rules are made explicit to students, they can and will learn them and will use them as tools to understand abstract concepts (Jamison). Students in SI sessions can write definitions of mathematical concepts, and the group can judge how accurate, precise, and complete the definitions are. The goal of some linked introductory college mathematics and rhetoric courses is to set out the "grammar of algebra" alongside the "grammar of rhetoric" so that students can conceive of math as more than just numbers and symbols but a language possessive of its own grammar (Heckelman & Dunn, 2003). Through this method, students learn that algebraic notation is a form of reasoning and that a particular notation usually denotes a specific course of action. SI sessions can help students understand that in learning math they are learning a new language by including not only the solving of mathematical equations in symbolic form, but the expository explanations that accompany them. This allows students to understand problems, as well as solve them. For this process, the boardwork model works well: one board is used for the mathematical solution and one for the narrative of the solution, along with expansive explanations of the concepts involved. Students should work on these in small groups or dyads.

Language also can be used to demystify word problems. Students can work in groups to free-write, brainstorm, cluster, and outline their thinking on problems. To do so, they will also have to practice very close reading. SI sessions before exams are a particularly good time to use matrices or other visual organizers to classify types of problems, necessary formulae, and variables that may be involved. Another useful strategy involves having a handout with a number of problems, with only a tiny space provided to work each problem. In this space, students can show the initial steps they would take without actually solving the problem (Kenny, 1995).

Group problem solving. Another strategy that helps students in mathematics is group problem-solving. A typical example would be to have one student be the problem-solver and the others, the listeners. The problem-solver attempts to verbalize all the steps in the problem, including reading the problem aloud and selecting the appropriate variables and drawings as needed. The listeners make sure the problem-solver constantly verbalizes and checks for accuracy. Each student takes a turn as the problem-solver. Another approach for problem solving is the Think-Pair-Share strategy (Lyman, 1981) in which a problem is posed by one of the group members or by the leader. Each student thinks about the problem, jotting down things if needed, but does not talk. Then students pair up to discuss the problem, and after a few minutes, each pair shares their solution and ideas with the larger group. Another collaborative, problem-solving strategy is for the leader to write problems on separate pieces of paper and pass them around in the group. One person begins the solution, passes the paper to the next, and so on. Invariably, along the way, students begin discussing the problems with each other by asking the former problem-solvers why they did what they did, or why they left out certain steps.

Visual representation. The use of graphics and drawings is crucial in mathematics and engineering SI sessions. Students often remark that the first time they understood quadratic equations was when they saw them solved on a graphing calculator or in mathematic software. Students need to see how the signs or numbers are manipulated. To check for understanding, the SI session should include an opportunity for students to do their own drawings and graphing. Graphs and visual representations are most effective when they include real-life situations (Koellner-Clark, Stallings, & Hoover, 2002). Many students complain that they will never use the mathematics they are learning once they are finished with their coursework. So, if an SI session can help students relate percentages to finding the best sale at Macy's, understand average versus instantaneous rate of change in grasping how the officer clocked them at 85 mph, or picture the concept of slope in terms of the difficulty levels of snow ski runs, then SI has been successful in relating mathematics to their life experiences.

Visual representations may also include models drawn from everyday life. Students can construct models—such as one depicting their family—and embed themselves within the structure (Heckelman & Dunn, 2003). They can use any graphical means: genograms, Venn diagrams, flow charts, or pictures. Students can compare their models to demonstrate alternative ideas. They can then translate their models into algebraic equations. Such modeling is also useful in applied mathematics (Perelman, 1999), where students need to answer questions such as, "Should we do X?" If so, they need to develop and answer more specific questions: "What is the present problem? How will X solve it? What are some alternative ways of approaching it? What are the costs and benefits?"

Note review is also useful in mathematics sessions. Often, students only write down the numbers from the problems on the board, leaving out the explanation. When they leave the lecture, they forget what the professor said about the numbers, how the equation was solved, why steps were circumvented or deleted, and/or why certain steps were taken. If students learn to write the numbers and symbols and what the professors said about them, they will have more success in the discipline. Then, once they approach expertise, they, too, can use shorthand notations.

Conclusion

The more we know about how students learn, the more we can share across disciplines, and the better we will be able to plan and conduct successful SI sessions. Though many of our strategies work in generalized ways across the disciplines, it does appear helpful that we focus on the individual characteristics of various fields as well. We should continue to learn about the tacit understandings of the disciplines and the implicit rules that govern them in order to help our students experience the most success in their pursuit of higher education.

References

Ackerman, J. (1991). Reading, writing, and knowing: The role of disciplinary knowledge in comprehending and composing. *Research in the Teaching of English, 25*, 133-178.

Baum-Brunner, S. (1997). Be not deceived: Looking at historians' and compositionists' views of multiculturalism in freshman composition courses. *Language and Learning Across the Disciplines, 2*(1), 85-95.

Bazerman, C. (1981). What written knowledge does: Three examples of academic discourse. *Philosophy of the Social Sciences, 11*, 361-387.

Bower, G. H., Clark, M., Lesgold, A. M., & Winzenz, D. (1969). Hierarchical retrieval schemes in recall of categorized word lists. *Journal of Verbal and Verbal Behavior, 8*, 323-343.

Chase, W. G., & Simon, H. A. (1973). The mind's eye in chess. In W. G. Chase (Ed.), *Visual information processing*. New York: Academic Press.

Chi, M. T. H., Feltovich, P. J., & Glaser, R. (1981). Categorization and representation of physics problems by experts and novices. *Cognitive Science, 5*, 121-152.

Chi, M. T. H., Glaser, R., & Rees, E. (1982). Expertise in problem solving. In R. J. Sternberg (Ed.), *Advances in the psychology of human intelligence* (Vol. 1, pp. 7-76). Hillsdale, NJ: Erlbaum.

Coppola, B. P., & Daniels, D. S. (1996). The role of written and verbal expression in improving communication skills for students in an undergraduate chemistry program. *Language and Learning Across the Disciplines, 1*(3), 67-86.

de Jong, T., & Ferguson-Hessler, M. C. M. (1996). Types and qualities of knowledge. *Educational Psychologist, 31*(2), 105-113.

Devitt, A. (1991). Intertextuality in tax accounting: Generic, referential, and functional. In C. Bazerman & J. Paradis (Eds.), *Textual dynamics of the professions: Historical and contemporary studies of writing in professional communities* (pp. 336-357). Madison, WI: University of Wisconsin Press.

Driskill, L., Lewis K., Stearns, J., & Volz, T. (1998). Students' reasoning and rhetorical knowledge in first-year chemistry. *Language and Learning Across the Disciplines, 2*(3), 3-24.

Durst, R. K. (1994). Coming to grips with theory: College students' use of theoretical explanation in writing about history. *Language and Learning Across the Disciplines, 1*(1), 72-87.

Geisler, C. (1994a). *Academic literacy and the nature of expertise: Reading, writing, and knowing in academic philosophy.* Hillsdale, NJ: Erlbaum.

Geisler, C. (1994b). Literacy and expertise in the academy. *Language and Learning Across the Disciplines, 1*(1), 35-57.

Glynn, S. M., Yeany, R. H., & Britton, B. K. (1991). A constructive view of learning science. In S. M. Glynn, R. H. Yeany, & B. K. Britton (Eds.), *The psychology of learning* (pp. 3-19), Hillsdale, NJ: Erlbaum.

Gonzales, P., Calsyn, C., Jocelyn, L., Mak, K., Kastberg, D., Arafeh, S., Williams, T., & Tsen, W. (2000). Pursuing excellence: Comparisons of international eighth-grade mathematics and science achievement from a U.S. perspective [Special Issue]. *Education Statistics Quarterly, 3*(1).

Heckelman, R. J., & Dunn, III, W. M. (2003). Models in algebra and rhetoric: A new approach to integrating writing and mathematics in a WAC learning community. *Language and Learning Across the Disciplines, 6*(3), 74-88.

Herrington, A. J. (1985a). Classrooms as forums for reasoning and writing. *College Composition and Communication, 36*, 404-413.

Herrington, A. J. (1985b). Writing in academic settings: A study of the contexts for writing in two college chemical engineering courses. *Research in the Teaching of English, 19*, 331-361.

Hoff, D. (1997, April 9). New images of teaching. *Education Week.* Retrieved January 23, 2006, from http://www.edweek.org/ew/articles/199704/09/28video1.h16.html?querystring+new

Hoff, D. (2001, April 11). A world-class education eludes man in the U. S. *Education Week.* Retrieved January 23, 2006, from http://www.edweek.org/ew/articles/2001/04/11/30timss.h20.html?querystring+world-class

Hynd, C. R. (1999). Teaching students to think critically using multiple texts in history. *Journal of Adolescent and Adult Literacy, 42*(6), 428-436.

Jamison, R. E. (2000). Learning the language of mathematics. *Language and Learning Across the Disciplines, 4*(1), 45-54.

Kaufer, D., & Young, R. (1993). Writing in the content areas. In L. Odell (Ed.), *Theory and practice in the teaching of writing: Rethinking the discipline* (pp. 71-104). Carbondale, IL: Southern Illinois University Press.

Kenny, P. (Speaker). (1995). *Dr. Pat Kenney on SI in mathematics* (Videotape). Kansas City, MO: University of Missouri–Kansas City.

Koellner-Clark, K., Stallings, L. L., & Hoover, S. A. (2002). Socratic seminars for mathematics. *Mathematics Teacher, 95*, 682-687.

Linton, P., Madigan, R., & Johnson, S. (1994). Introducing students to disciplinary genres: The role of the general composition course. *Language and Learning Across the Disciplines, 1*(2), 63-78.

Lyman, F. (1981). ReadingQuest strategies: Think-pair-share. Retrieved January 24, 2006, from http://curry.edschool.virginia.edu/go/readquest/strat/tps.html

Manzo, A. V. (1969). The request procedure. *Journal of Reading, 13*, 123-126.

Meltzer, D. E. (2005). Relation between students' problem-solving performance and representational format. *American Journal of Physics, 73*(5), 463-478.

Perelman, L. C. (1999). The two rhetorics: Design and interpretation in engineering and humanistic discourse. *Language and Learning Across the Disciplines, 3*(2), 64-82.

Redish, E. F., & Steinberg, R. N. (1999). Teaching physics: Figuring out what works. *Physics Today, 52*, 24-30.

Robertson, W. C. (1990). Detection of cognitive structure with protocol data: Predicting performance on physics transfer problems. *Cognitive Science, 14*, 253-280.

Shahn, E., & Costello, R. K. (2000). Evidence and interpretation: Teachers' reflections on reading and writing in an introductory science course. *Language and Learning Across the Disciplines, 4*(2), 47-82.

Spiegel, G. F., & Barufaldi, J. P. (1994). The effects of a combination of text structure awareness and graphic post organizers on recall and retention of science knowledge. *Journal of Research in Science Teaching, 31*(9), 913-932.

Stockton, S. (1994). Students and professionals writing biology: Disciplinary work and apprentice storytellers. *Language and Learning Across the Disciplines, 1*(2), 79-104.

University of Missouri – Kansas City. (2004). *Supplemental Instruction leader resource manual.* Kansas City, MO: The Curators of the University of Missouri.

Walvoord, B., & McCarthy, L. P. (1990). *Thinking and writing in college: A naturalistic study of students in four disciplines.* Urbana, IL: National Council of Teachers of English.

Wilkins, H. (1990, March). *Learning to write at work: Responses to the writing of junior engineers.* Paper presented at the College Composition and Communication Conference, Chicago, IL.

Wineburg, S. S. (1991). On the reading of historical texts: Notes on the breach between school and academy. *American Educational Research Journal, 28*(3), 495-519.

Chapter 7

Video-Based Supplemental Instruction

Maureen Hurley, Kay Patterson, Sonny Painter, and Jennifer Carnicom

Video-based Supplemental Instruction (VSI)—an outgrowth of Supplemental Instruction—is an interactive information delivery system that helps students master course content as they develop and refine reasoning and learning skills. In VSI courses, instructors record their entire semester's sequence of lectures in a studio, which are then made available on videotape (note: the term videotape will be used throughout this chapter to represent any and all formats in which a lecture may be recorded). Students can then enroll in a VSI section of the class, using these videotaped lectures, if they are so advised. The instructor also holds a live section of the identical course offering during the same semester; students enrolled in the live lecture section and students enrolled in the VSI section cover all of the same material and take all of the same exams. A trained facilitator uses these taped lectures to regulate the flow of information to the learner. The lectures are stopped and started as needed, allowing the facilitator to verify that students have understood one idea before moving on to the next. Students develop essential reading, learning, and study skills, while they master course content in core curriculum subjects.

This chapter provides an overview of VSI, including the impetus for its development, fundamental program elements, data outcomes, and adaptations of the model. Special attention is paid to the structure of the VSI model and the academic results for university students enrolled in history, math, and chemistry VSI courses. The chapter also examines how VSI works in other settings and suggests future directions for the model.

Need for VSI

In the early 1990s, a greater number of underprepared students were enrolling at the University of Missouri – Kansas City. It became clear that an additional delivery system of academic support, besides SI, was needed for some students (Martin & Blanc, 1994). SI Staff found that successful students were able to perform three tasks well: (a) understand the lectures, (b) take adequate notes, and (c) demonstrate their competency through assignments and exams. Therefore, the VSI model was developed to guide underprepared students in developing these skills. All of an instructor's course lectures were recorded, and a facilitator was selected to guide the students in their learning. They could ask to have the lectures stopped when they needed clarification or more time to write meaningful notes. The facilitator checked for understanding, to be certain students had mastered difficult concepts. The students in the VSI class met four to five days a week in two-hour blocks, allowing them more time on task and the opportunity to work continually in small collaborative learning groups.

Early in the development of the VSI program, Deanna Martin, founder of both SI and VSI, spent a great deal of time nurturing relationships with administrators, faculty, and staff to get the VSI pilot off the ground. Funding for the courses was provided from existing budgets. Her knowledge of learning, gained from working with students in professional schools (i.e., medical, dental, and pharmacy schools), helped in the development of the early VSI classes. Other staff also provided leadership for the program. That consistency gave the program stability, and relationships were forged throughout the institution.

When VSI was developed, administrators, department chairs, deans, and faculty supported the initiative. The program won credibility when, early on, it was found that students who enrolled in VSI classes performed at or above the rate of students in the non-VSI section of the course and that D, F, and withdrawal (DFW) rates of VSI students were lower than those in the non-VSI sections. Administrators saw VSI as a tool to retain students whose academic backgrounds might otherwise prevent them from doing well in their classes.

Tinto (1993) believes that students must feel integrated into higher education, both academically and socially, in order to succeed. Yet, many students experience isolation. The small class size and student interaction of VSI courses is one way to combat this. Moreover, research shows that when students are placed in small groups, they accomplish deeper, more meaningful learning. A small-group model provides greater critical thinking opportunities than when students work in isolation (Martin & Blanc, 1994; Sadler & Whimbey, 1985).

How VSI Differs from the SI Model

While VSI and SI use similar strategies, several features distinguish them. SI study sessions are held outside of class and are attached to traditionally difficult courses with a student SI leader conducting the sessions. The SI sessions focus on learning strategies that students can practice and apply to understanding and organizing critical course content. The VSI model integrates learning strategies directly into the course, using the instructor's recorded lectures. A trained facilitator leads these small class sessions, which are held two hours a day, five days a week. Students spend more time practicing strategies and solving problems in a VSI class than they do in an SI session (which usually lasts 50 minutes). Both SI and VSI use learning techniques specific to a discipline and actively engage students in learning. Participants work together and teach each other by way of processing and reporting back. Planning for sessions and training facilitators are also important to both models.

While SI leaders are often undergraduate students who have been successful in the target course, VSI facilitators are usually graduate students, but can be undergraduate students or sometimes staff members. In both SI and VSI, leaders and facilitators must be approved by the professor. Since students meet for 10 hours per week with a facilitator in VSI, they can more deeply engage with difficult course content. The professor's lectures are often produced with built-in stopping points that provide opportunities for the facilitator to ask probing questions and model critical thinking strategies. Students frequently work in small groups to discuss the lecture content. Though many students find that SI meets their needs, underprepared students may benefit more from VSI due to the extra time to think about and process information with their classmates.

VSI Program Structure

There are two major components to VSI: (a) the lecture content, contributed by the course professor, and (b) the critical-thinking and learning strategies, managed by the facilitator. In the lecture component, the instructor delivers the recorded lectures, creates assessment materials, and establishes the criteria for grading. In VSI, students also co-enroll in a separate, critical-thinking course. Both courses are delivered simultaneously and students receive three credit hours for each of the courses, equaling six credit hours. Strategies to assist students in learning the material more effectively are directly embedded into the processing of course content. The facilitator assumes the task of ensuring that students understand and learn the course content. The facilitator or a student can stop the tape so that students can clarify their notes, ask questions, and discuss concepts. If students are struggling with notetaking, the facilitator can model effective strategies or have a student who has mastered notetaking demonstrate his or her technique.

In a problem-solving class such as chemistry or math, VSI students practice solving difficult problems when the tape is stopped by applying what they have seen the professor demonstrate in the taped lecture. In a VSI information-based course such as history, the stops can be used to organize information in a meaningful way. The facilitator constantly observes students, looking for signs of confusion, and asks questions that help students recall, think about, and apply new information. Students are often placed in small groups and given a task that allows them the opportunity to think critically and discuss difficult course content.

In a VSI class, the facilitator uses a variety of strategies. Novice learners may lack the maturity to complete some assignments, so in a VSI class, there are frequent checks to make sure that assignments are understood and completed. The facilitator checks all the assignments and quizzes. Students' participation in class is also part of the grade students receive in the critical thinking course that is linked to the content.

Selecting and Training Facilitators

The selection and training of facilitators is critical. The professor plays a key role in recommending facilitators, who are often graduate students in the discipline. The selection process involves an interview, a demonstration by the candidate of a sample VSI lesson, feedback from the VSI coordinator, and a second demonstration incorporating the feedback. The VSI program coordinator looks for good communication skills and the ability to take suggestions and make adjustments.

Training of facilitators by the coordinator is comprehensive and ongoing (i.e., biweekly training and coaching sessions are held). The focus of the initial training is on managing groups, planning activities, communicating learning strategies, and checking for understanding.

VSI Elements

Several important elements make VSI sessions effective. Time to think occurs when the lecture is stopped. This allows students the opportunity to formulate questions, discuss key concepts, and share ideas with other students. Managed study time is important for underprepared or novice learners. The facilitator can organize the class in such a way that allows students to grapple with difficult concepts and engage more deeply with the course content. Focus on student control is quite different than the method often used in a traditional lecture class where the emphasis is on the instructor teaching. Students find it easy to be passive notetakers without really thinking about the lecture. VSI places the students in the center of the learning process. They preview each lecture by focusing on the topic and discussing what may be contained in lecture. They identify key components, practice developing and predicting questions, and control the pace of their learning.

One of the goals of VSI is to give control of the lesson to the students and make them responsible for their own learning. To achieve this, the VSI methodology consists of four important elements that make the sessions effective: (a) preview, (b) process, (c) review, and (d) polish. Each element allows the students to take some ownership in the learning process.

Preview is used to get the attention of the students. The facilitator uses this technique to determine students' prior knowledge of a subject, discuss unfamiliar vocabulary, and cover the main ideas of the lecture. The preview is also used to ease the students into the lecture by lowering their anxiety about unfamiliar material. Preview activities might include defining vocabulary words from the lecture, discussing questions from the text in small groups, or brainstorming to determine prior knowledge. The most difficult part of the preview is the management of time. It is crucial for students to stay caught up with the readings and lecture notes and come to class prepared. Sometimes, peers can motivate each other if they are frequently required to engage in small-group discussions and report back what they have discussed.

In science and math courses, students can read sections of a chapter before the lecture is presented in order to become familiar with new vocabulary and to see how the effective use of the textbook can help them understand the material. By reading ahead in learning materials developed for the course, students can also focus on information which may help them better understand the lecture. Another technique for previewing in a math or science VSI class is to give each small group of students a new term or equation from an upcoming lecture or a review term from past lectures that relate to new information. Students spend two to three minutes discussing the content and write their ideas about the concept or equation on a white board.

Process. Processing information from the lecture is central to VSI. Students view the lecture for a short time, and it is stopped to allow them time to discuss important points or ask questions of each other. The facilitator needs to determine when and how often to stop the lecture. She/he should sit among the students, take notes, and observe, asking him/herself, "Do the students look confused? Are they writing too much or not enough?" These are cues to stop the lecture for discussion. Stops should also occur when the professor has moved on to a new concept.

A fundamental aspect of VSI is students teaching each other. Redirecting questions back to the group allows students time to think about an answer and explain their ideas to others. Wait-time goes hand-in-hand with redirecting questions. This is the time between asking a question and getting a response. It also allows students time to process the question before answering. In addition, there should be wait time between students' answers and the asking of new questions. This encourages students to build on information and/or offer more clarification. Students can rely on one another as additional resources.

In both VSI math and chemistry courses, a sufficient amount of information has to be presented before much processing can occur. Students should first consider what the preview stage revealed to them about what they know or do not know. In processing, the facilitator can have students try to solve a problem and spend a few minutes struggling with it. Then, the lecture can be continued, and students can learn an effective way to solve the problem. Above all, students need to understand the reasoning that the lecturer used to approach the problem. Often, facilitators will manage the lecture by asking students to solve sample problems before the lecturer solves similar ones. If students appear lost, the facilitator can allow several of the problems to be presented by the lecturer. An important technique is for the facilitator to stop the content flow often enough that students have an opportunity to try to solve problems on their own and discuss their reasoning and solutions with their peers.

To be skillful in the processing stage, the facilitator must observe students to see if they are confused or if they are asking each other questions. The facilitator can then stop the lecture and ask a student to explain a problem. If students show that they understand, the facilitator can give an extra problem for students to solve individually and then initiate a group discussion to verify their understanding. During processing, the facilitator should listen, ask questions, and demonstrate how he or she thinks through working problems.

An important technique to use during this phase is a boardwork model, which emphasizes setting up problems so that students can show their reasoning processes. This model includes listing prerequisites needed to work problems (e.g., formulas and equations), steps needed to work the problem, rules along with a narrative description of steps, and the creation of a new problem (to illustrate mastery). Boardwork helps provide visual information to help students better understand the process. The facilitator can construct a table or graph with information in a matrix and guide the students in the problem-solving process. Asking students to explore certain questions before they start solving a problem and knowing what the problem is asking also helps them understand how to begin working a problem. The facilitator can reinforce the method the lecturer is using and set the expectation that students will show their work in an organized and well-reasoned way.

Review. After students view and discuss the lecture or textbook chapters, they need to review what they have learned. This stage allows more opportunities for the facilitator to check for understanding. A quick note review can be used and is very helpful to students. Concept maps and matrices developed on lecture topics demonstrate relationships between concepts and ideas. Ideally, review should occur within each class period. Once the lecture has been viewed and students have filled in the gaps in their notes, the material should be discussed and tied to previous content. A review at the beginning of class is also very helpful. This can be conducted informally in a large group, or students can work together in small groups. A sample review activity is a vocabulary development exercise in which the facilitator chooses three or four words for students to explain the meaning and significance. Once students have completed this activity in small groups, they share their definitions with the rest of the class.

Review in a VSI math or VSI chemistry class can take many forms. It may occur at the beginning of class to clarify homework difficulties, or it may take place once information has been presented and students begin to understand the work. The facilitator must keep the group on track. A good technique is to have students list problems that are most difficult for them. Students who understand those problems can demonstrate how to solve them. If they are given the opportunity to explain to someone else how they solved the problem, their learning is reinforced. If no one can solve a given problem, the facilitator can model one and then give students a similar problem to work out.

Polish is an extension of review and helps students with final exam preparation. It allows them to reorganize information into various categories. Some in-class polishing activities might include writing practice essays, predicting and formulating practice test questions, and testing one another. The facilitator may have to coach students on how to predict questions and give examples. As the course continues, students should start to develop their own exam reviews. Students can grade their own papers, as peers demonstrate and explain how to solve the problems. Games (e.g., Jeopardy) that are created using lecture material are also effective polishing strategies, especially when small groups of students write their own questions. To help those who are visual, rather than auditory learners, the facilitator can design a version of hangman or pictionary to learn the vocabulary.

After each exam, students should complete a post-exam debriefing, which enables them to think about why some of their answers were incorrect. Students look at each question and determine if they misread the questions or choices, failed to learn details, or did not study or read the right material. This method can help students determine how successful their learning and study strategies were and whether they need to change them.

Outcomes

VSI classes are evaluated by academic outcomes. As increasing numbers of underprepared students are admitted to the university, greater challenges exist in supporting the needs of these students. Since VSI classes began to be offered in the early 1990s, mean final course grades for VSI students have frequently been equal to or greater than those of non-VSI students with comparable student profiles. The DFW rates are also important indicators of program success, as they have implications for student retention. Data from UMKC's VSI program were collected from fall 1997 through fall 2005 for Chemistry 211 (general chemistry) and History 201 (Western civilization). Data from the VSI section of Mathematics 110 (intermediate algebra) were collected from fall 1999 through fall 2005. Given that entering ACT scores of non-VSI students are higher than their VSI counterparts (Figures 1, 3, and 5), one would predict that they would have lower DFW rates, but just the opposite is often true. Figures 2, 4, and 6 show a comparison of the grades earned by VSI students versus non-VSI students in chemistry, history, and mathematics, respectively. The percentage of VSI students receiving a DFW grade was lower than that of the non-VSI students in all three disciplines. Additionally, in chemistry, the VSI group's grades actually surpassed those of the non-VSI group. In Western civilization, they were the same, even though the VSI group had lower ACT scores entering college.

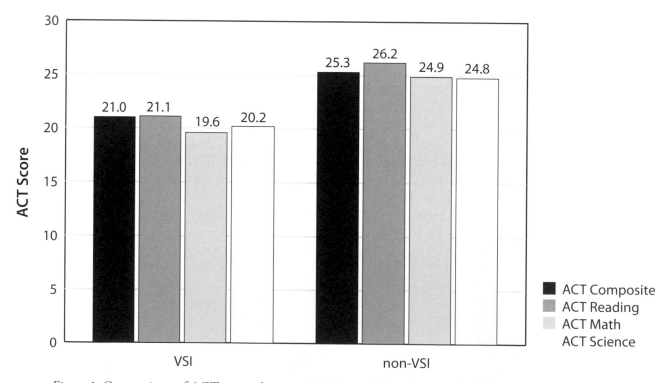

Figure 1. Comparison of ACT scores between VSI (*n* = 290) and non-VSI Chemistry 211 students (*n* = 2,938), 1997 - 2005.

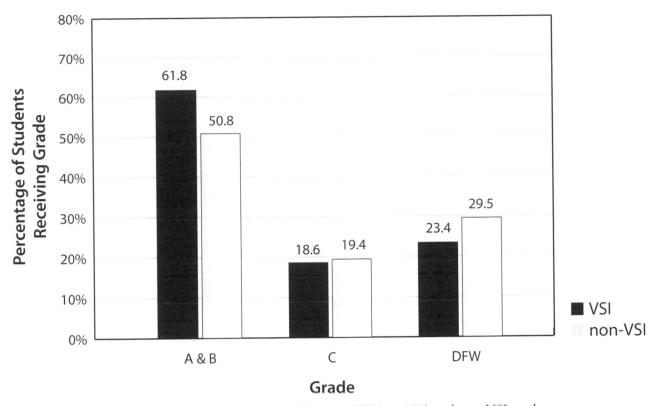

Figure 2. Comparison of Chemistry 211 grades between VSI (*n* = 290) and non-VSI students (*n* = 2,938), 1997 - 2005.

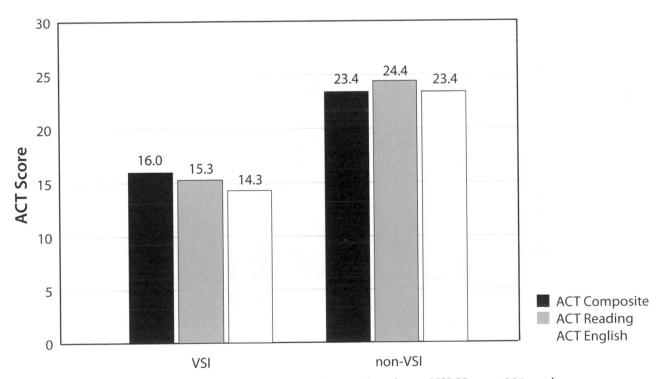

Figure 3. Comparison of ACT scores between VSI (*n* = 322) and non-VSI History 201 students (*n* = 1,679), 1997 - 2005.

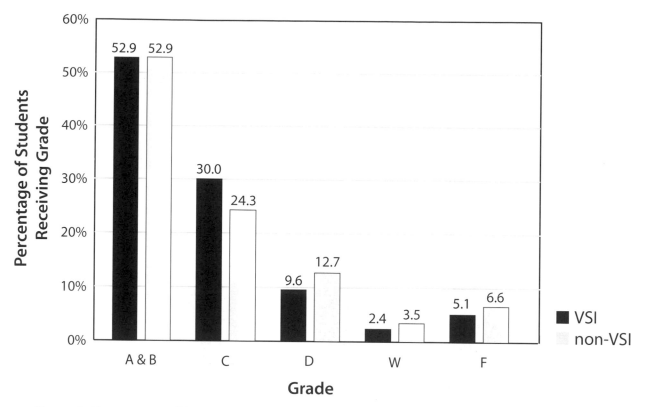

Figure 4. Comparison of History 201 grades between VSI (*n* = 322) and non-VSI students (*n* = 1,679), 1997 - 2005.

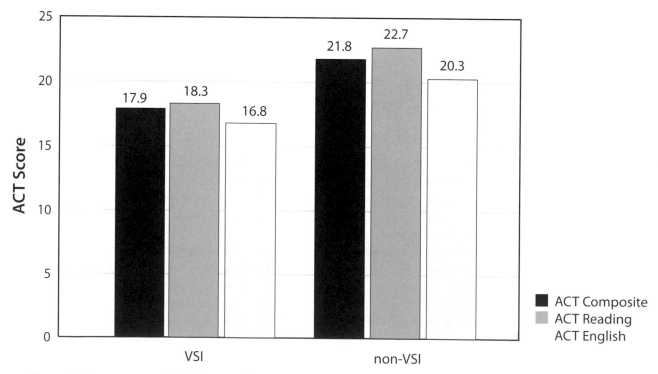

Figure 5. Comparison of ACT scores between VSI (*n* = 533) and non-VSI Math 110 students (*n* = 2,871), 1999-2005.

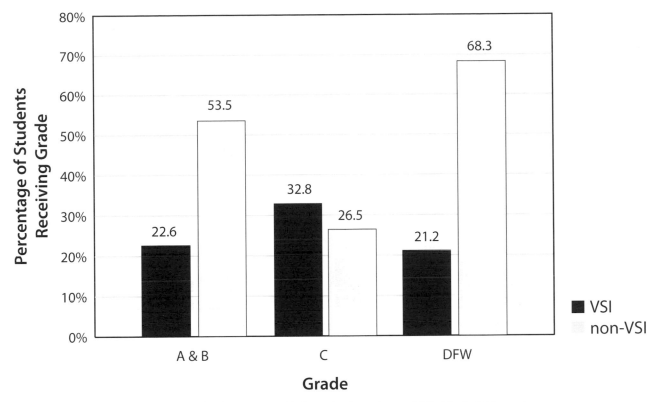

Figure 6. Comparison of grades between VSI (*n* = 533) and non-VSI Math 110 students (*n* = 2,871), 1999 - 2005.

Adaptations of VSI

VSI has proven effective in helping increase student retention. Because of that, the program has been adapted to meet the needs of several other populations.

VSI Dual-Enrollment High School Adaptation

Representatives from rural Missouri high schools contacted UMKC in the mid-1990s requesting a distance-learning offering for their students. As data continued to reflect positive outcomes for students enrolled in campus VSI courses, an adaptation of the model appeared to be appropriate for use in those schools. Therefore, a VSI model was developed that could easily be administered off-campus to serve a population of college-bound, high school students.

Since 1994, VSI staff has offered dual-enrollment courses to rural high schools in Missouri. These schools particularly benefit from VSI courses since they do not always have certified teachers with master's degrees—a mandate required by the Missouri Department of Secondary Education to teach certain courses. Since a professor's content is captured on video and he or she controls the curriculum and evaluation of the course, high school teachers can use the lectures and concentrate on managing the learning. This modified distance-education class also allows students to earn both university and high school credit.

Implementing a dual-enrollment program required changes in the VSI course delivery. In order for high school students to be successful in a college course, the course time needed to be extended. In the majority of high schools that offer VSI courses, the courses are completed in two semesters, rather than one. This follows the on-campus model of doubling the time in class to allow for content presentation and processing of information. Instead of two-hour blocks, five days a week, for 16 weeks, high schools offer the course over an entire school year, one hour a day, and five days a week.

One modification to the high school VSI chemistry course is an on-campus (UMKC) lab component, since many rural schools do not have the facilities, materials, or expertise to offer the required labs. To meet the requirement of the one-hour lab component, students must attend two on-campus chemistry labs, which are held on Saturdays. Students prepare for the labs before they come to campus to expedite the process. The professor, with the help of many assistants, oversees the execution of these services.

Providing ample resources for the facilitators/teachers and students in the high school program is essential. As in the on-campus model, the VSI dual-enrollment program offers training to support the facilitators/teachers. Schools that implement VSI are required to send their teachers who will be facilitating the VSI courses, to an intensive, two-day training each year. The training workshop covers not only the logistics of administering the courses, but also the learning strategies associated with the VSI model. Facilitators/teachers are given additional support materials developed by the VSI program that incorporate the learning strategies of the VSI model into the lecture, as well as text materials provided by the course professor. Facilitators/teachers also have access to online resource materials developed by VSI staff as well as e-mail and phone support. To further assists the facilitators/teachers and ensure proper training and implementation of the VSI courses into the schools, VSI staff visits the high schools to observe classroom facilitators/teachers and offer feedback.

High school students participating in VSI courses also have many resources available to them. Not only do they have the trained facilitator/teacher to help them learn the material, they also have a manual developed by VSI staff that incorporates learning strategies into the course content. An additional online component offers quizzes and practice exams. Students are able to correspond with the professor via e-mail or when they visit the UMKC campus.

The adaptation of VSI courses to provide dual-credit opportunities for high school students has many benefits. From the university perspective, an additional revenue stream occurs from the leasing of materials and from the tuition and fees of students taking the course for college credit. VSI courses also introduce students to the university, which provides a cost-effective recruiting opportunity. As for the benefits for high schools, their administrators can offer dual-enrollment courses in their curriculum without having to employ certified instructors with master's degrees. The asynchronous delivery of the VSI courses allows for easy integration of the class into the high school course schedule. Benefits for the teachers include an easy way to integrate effective collaborative learning strategies, as the VSI curriculum is already developed. Teachers spend less time preparing for content delivery, allowing more time to focus on student learning. They also do not have to create and grade exams, as those tasks are handled by the university professor of record. The primary beneficiaries are the students, who develop new and effective learning strategies, which can also be applied to other classes. They can earn inexpensive college credit, as well as meet their requirements toward high school graduation. This adaptation of the VSI program continues to be well-received and has yielded positive results in final course grades for rural high school students.

VSI Calculus I Adaptation

UMKC students and math department faculty approached the Center for Academic Development with an interest in developing a VSI Calculus I course for nonmathematics majors. A course was developed, and the funding was secured. The VSI Calculus I course differed in several ways from other VSI offerings. The targeted population differed from the students usually served by our VSI courses in that the group included juniors and seniors, students with average to above-average ACT scores, and students pursuing entrance into professional degree programs at UMKC. Because this population was more accustomed to the rigors of college work, the in-class time commitment for this course was abbreviated. Historically, UMKC VSI courses have been designed to meet two hours a day, five days a week in order to incorporate the presentation of lectures on tape and the processing of content by students. However, the new VSI Calculus I course was developed to do all this in one hour a day, five days a week.

This time-in-class modification required the addition of optional (but recommended) study sessions, offering an additional five hours on task per week. This allowed for more processing and practicing of content, which follows the SI model. Students were not required to attend the additional study sessions, although many did take advantage of this opportunity to practice solving more problems and have their questions answered. The structure of the class remained the same as other VSI courses in that it included preview, process, review, and polish components and was limited in size.

The VSI Calculus I course was piloted in the fall 2005 semester and its outcomes ($n = 9$, one class) were compared to two groups of students. One group, the control ($n = 75$, two classes), covered the same subject matter and was given the same exams as the VSI section They were taught in a traditional, lecture-style format from a popular instructor different from the instructor on the videos. The final group consisted of the remainder of the students who enrolled in Calculus I at UMKC that semester ($n = 103$, four classes). These students (who included mathematics majors and medical/pharmacy/dental students) were exposed to a variety of testing and lecture styles that were determined by the individual instructors of the sections. Figure 7 shows the breakdown of Calculus I course grades across the three groups.

The results from the fall 2005 pilot VSI Calculus I course demonstrate that the VSI learning environment greatly impacts students' success. The goal of the VSI Calculus project was for students

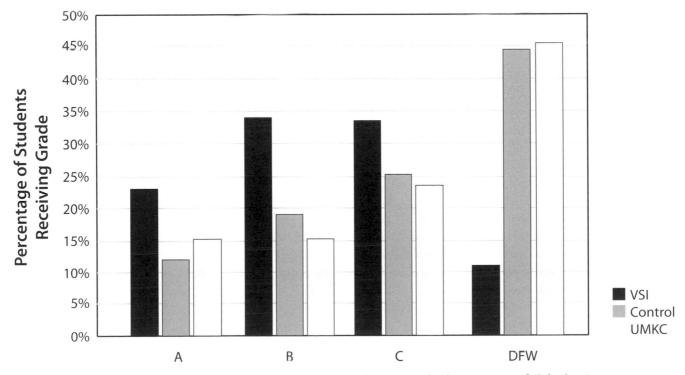

Figure 7. Grades of VSI participants compared to control group and other sections of Calculus I.

enrolled in the VSI section of Calculus I to excel in mastering the content and for the DFW rate to not exceed 25%, enabling students to continue on in their majors and graduate. The VSI students (Mean GPA = 2.91) received higher grades than the control group (Mean GPA = 1.44, p = 0.053), and that of the other UMKC students (Mean GPA = 2.016, p = 0.069). The DFW percentage (11.1%) for VSI students was considerably lower than that of the control group (44.0%, p = 0.061) and was also lower than the other UMKC students (45.6%, p = 0.046) for Calculus I. The results from the pilot exceeded our expectations.

VSI at Other Institutions

During the same time period, the UMKC staff was asked to develop courses using the VSI learning model for the former University of Port Elizabeth in South Africa (now Nelson Mandela Metropolitan University), as that university had already been successful with SI on their campus. It was thought that the development of VSI classes in various subjects would help address the needs of the majority Black South African students who had been deprived of higher educational opportunities during apartheid. With the transformation occurring, there lay ahead the daunting task of attempting to redress grievances and somehow begin to level the academic playing field for thousands of citizens needing basic, as well as advanced, educational skills (Hurley, 2000). Partners in the project included a local community outreach center associated with University of Port Elizabeth (UPE), the resulting community college that grew out of the community center, a local South African foundation, UPE, and the University of Missouri – Kansas City.

Courses were developed in mathematics, accounting, chemistry, and physiology. The VSI group in mathematics (a gatekeeper course in South Africa) has performed equally or better than the live lecture group on all of the exams. Outcomes in accounting and physiology have shown approximately equal mean performance levels for underprepared students in the off-campus VSI program and those regularly admitted on-campus in the live lecture class. The chemistry class had different results. The department presented fewer lectures for the VSI tapes, with an average length of 25 minutes, compared to 55 minutes for the regular lecture. No advanced preparation for exams was included in the videotapes, though it was provided in the regular lecture. The VSI students performed nearly as well as their peers in on-campus sections (though below the VSI program staff's expectations). Despite this mixed performance, VSI looks promising as a viable part of programming to redress shortfalls in tertiary education in South Africa.

For the past several years, VSI has also been used at various high schools in Sweden. UMKC staff has assisted in training high school teachers in mathematics classes in the VSI model. Faculty and students from Lund University (Lund, Sweden) have continued to partner with secondary school teachers in using VSI strategies in classes and in study sessions. A course in mechanics was produced and provided for usage in the various high schools.

Conclusion

VSI allows students in the classroom, with the guidance of a facilitator, to exercise greater control over three areas that influence learning: (a) the amount of time on task, (b) the structure of the presentation of content, and (c) the amount of interaction in the classroom. How VSI benefits each of these areas is summarized as follows. In addition to providing students with more time on task, VSI enables students to control the pace of the instruction. VSI integrates critical thinking and study skills and captures and helps manage students' study time. Moreover, VSI allows students to earn additional college credit through dual enrollment in a companion study skills course. Finally, VSI builds an expectation for processing material with others, thereby promoting understanding rather than memorizing important course content.

Future plans for VSI at UMKC include the development of additional sections to support other courses in the natural and social sciences, mathematics, and foreign languages. The UMKC Coaching Program, a new mentoring program that serves first-year and transfer students, will use a VSI course in fall 2008 to provide in-depth learning experiences for their students.

Opportunities are being looked at for expansion of VSI into other countries such as Grenada and India, whose rural masses do not have access to quality educational opportunities. Innovative learning experiences for such underserved populations could be created through the distance-learning aspects of the model.

References

Hurley, M. (2000). Video-based Supplemental Instruction (VSI): An interactive delivery system that facilitates student learning [Dissertation, University of Missouri – Kansas City, 1999]. *Dissertation Abstracts International, 61*(04), 1317.

Martin, D. C., & Blanc, R. (1994). VSI: A pathway to mastery and persistence. In D. C. Martin & D. Arendale (Eds.), *Supplemental Instruction: Increasing achievement and retention* (pp. 83-91). San Francisco: Jossey-Bass.

Sadler, Jr., W. A., & Whimbey, A. (1985). A holistic approach to improving thinking skills. *Phi Delta Kappan, 67*(3), 199-203.

Tinto, V. (1993). *Leaving college: Rethinking the causes and cures of student attrition* (2nd ed.). Chicago: The University of Chicago Press.

Chapter 8

Supplemental Instruction: International Adaptations and Future Directions

Glen Jacobs, M. Lisa Stout, and Marion E. Stone

Since its debut at the University of Missouri – Kansas City (UMKC) in 1973, Supplemental Instruction (SI) has expanded from a promising academic support model in the American Midwest into an international network that influences global scholarship and education. Adaptable and dynamic, the SI model lends itself to a number of innovative applications, some of which are currently in place and others that are on the horizon. In the 35 years since its development, international collaboration has played a key role in the growth of SI. As part of this collaboration, one of the main contributors to SI's expansion has been the strong training component for educators made available to participating institutions. Faculty and staff from more than 1,500 institutions representing 29 countries have attended UMKC-sponsored SI training workshops. Such trainings are the basis for meaningful dialogue on a worldwide scale. Within the presence of cultural differences, the shared value of global education provides a strong foundation for collaborative professional relationships among all of our SI colleagues.

International Adaptations

Early on, SI's founders decided that the SI model should be modified by its users rather than its creators. Martin and Blanc (1994) argue that SI should be "fluid rather than rigid, dynamic rather than static" (p. 92). As intended, the SI model has proven to be very versatile, and this is a primary reason why SI has been able to expand globally. The SI model has been adapted, using innovative strategies, to meet the distinct needs of cultures and educational systems that differ widely in philosophy, culture, budget, and student population. Despite these differences, all can incorporate the core components of SI into their individual organizations.

To demonstrate possible variations of the model and to illustrate innovative program ideas, five institutions from five different countries are highlighted in this chapter: (a) University of Manchester, United Kingdom; (b) University of Wollongong, Australia; (c) St. George's University, School of Medicine, Grenada, West Indies; (d) Nelson Mandela Metropolitan University, South Africa; and (e) Lund

University, Sweden. While these countries have unique educational systems, all have the commonality of having high-risk courses. The differences among these SI programs are described, and the benefits of their unique approaches are also noted.

University of Manchester, United Kingdom

The University of Manchester is a research-active institution resulting from the merger of two of Britain's foremost educational institutions, The Victoria University of Manchester and the University of Manchester Institute of Science and Technology. Created in 2004, the University of Manchester's roots date back to the early 1800s (University of Manchester, n.d.a). With more than 36,000 students and 10,000 staff members, the University of Manchester has four faculties (or colleges): Engineering and Physical Science, Humanities, Life Sciences, and Medical and Human Science (University of Manchester, n.d.b).

To assist students academically and to encourage student interaction with peers, the SI model was first introduced to the university in 1995. The SI program at the University of Manchester is referred to as PASS (peer-assisted study sessions), an acronym that serves as a marketing tool to imply that students are more likely to pass or progress into the next level of study if they participate in the program (Coe, McDougall, & McKeown, 1999).

First used in the chemistry department because of a combined 20% failure and drop-out rate of first-year students (Coe et al., 1999), PASS is currently available in 10 disciplines: chemistry, chemical engineering, civil engineering, computer science, life sciences, mathematics, Middle Eastern studies, Middle English, music, and physics. To promote higher attendance, students are automatically assigned to a PASS group. The assignment to a PASS group creates an expectation of participation and, therefore, increases attendance because the students have to make a conscious decision to 'opt out' rather than 'opt in' (W. Carey, personal communication, February 24, 2006).

One of the most unique aspects of this program relates to the PASS leaders. The University of Manchester's PASS program currently has 250 leaders, which is a large number compared to most SI programs. Additionally, contrary to most SI programs, these leaders are not paid. In fact, the reputation of PASS is such that it is highly desirable to be a leader despite the lack of monetary compensation. PASS leaders realize that there are other, greater rewards to be gained by the experience. It is well-documented that leaders increase their understanding of the subject material, improve their leadership and teamwork skills, and enhance their overall personal and professional growth (Ashwin, 1994; Donelan, 1999; Stone, Jacobs, & Hayes, 2006; Wallace, 1992). In addition, the experience gained by PASS leaders can be quite attractive to potential employers. According to William Carey, Students as Partners Officer,

> Employers place a huge emphasis and value on the skills [students] develop in their role, which is demonstrated by the sponsorship from a leading blue-chip, graduate employer. They support numerous aspects of the work and most notably offer a course, 'Personal Development and Effectiveness Training,' specifically for PASS Leaders. (personal communication, February 24, 2006).

In another interesting deviation from the traditional SI model, PASS leaders work in pairs at the University of Manchester. The PASS staff members have found that this is advantageous to the students attending the sessions and to the leaders themselves. For example, students benefit from the different skills, perspectives, and experiences individual leaders bring, and leaders are able to support each other and divide tasks during the sessions (W. Carey, personal communication, February 24, 2006).

The PASS program at the University of Manchester has demonstrated its success on many levels with the majority of this success derived from the strong partnership between the leaders and members of staff. The basis of this partnership is a strong commitment to student ownership; PASS is 'student owned, student led.' Since the leaders have recently experienced their own first year, they can identify the challenging situations facing new students most effectively. Working with staff, leaders (student coordinators) with at least one year of PASS experience develop the scheme on a yearly basis to adapt to the needs of new first-year students. Manchester has found that empowering the leaders in this way has a positive impact on the scheme and can lead to a change in student culture (Garside, Embury, & Carey, 2006). Participation in the program is very high. For example, sessions for some disciplines (e.g., Middle Eastern studies, chemical and civil engineering) boast attendance rates as high as 90%. To further document its impact, research has shown a grade increase of 12% for students who attend PASS compared to those who do not participate (Coe et al., 1999). A more recent study (Fostier, Sheffield, & Speake, 2006) showed a potential grade increase of 10% on the subject for which PASS was available and highlighted further qualitative benefits identified by first-year students when evaluating their reasons for attending PASS sessions, notably 'Understanding the course' (70%) and 'Preparation for assessment' (40%).

University of Wollongong, Australia

Formally established in 1975, the University of Wollongong (UOW) has more than 18,000 students and 1,600 staff members. Located in New South Wales, the university spans three campuses and incorporates five satellite centers. Known for its strong research programs, the university has academic courses in the following nine faculties: Arts, Education, Health & Behavioral Sciences, Engineering, Law, Science, Informatics, Commerce, and Creative Arts.

Over the years, UOW has attempted to establish different types of mentoring and peer-based programs, but they all quickly disappeared (S. Rogan, personal communication, February 13, 2006). This, however, was not the fate of the SI program at UOW, which was implemented in 2002 and, like at the University of Manchester, is commonly referred to as PASS (peer-assisted study sessions). Although a relatively young program, it has already proven itself with innovative ideas and data to support its success. Data indicate that regular PASS participants—those who attend five or more times—on average score higher final marks than nonparticipants (UOW, 2003-2004),[1] and international students who attended PASS regularly achieved final marks that were 20 points higher than nonparticipants (UOW, 2002-2003).[2]

One unique strategy used by the PASS program is to encourage students to formally enroll in a section of PASS. As part of an administrative and marketing plan, when students enroll in a class or lab, they can also enroll in PASS if it is offered for the course. Students who enroll in PASS seem to feel a greater commitment to participate, which appears to increase the likelihood of attendance (S. Rogan, personal communication, February 22, 2006). This strategy has proven to be effective, and attendance rates are very high. However, in the spirit of the original SI model, PASS program participation remains voluntary and open to all students in the supported class (S. Rogan, personal communication, February 26, 2006). Additionally, course credit and grades are not given to PASS participants for attendance, although there is a high probability that their class grade will be enhanced. In fact, it has been shown that students who participate in PASS have much higher pass rates than those who do not participate. These pass rates are particularly high for those students who attend 10 or more sessions per semester (Zerger, 2005).

PASS leaders often facilitate sessions in the following subjects at UOW: economics, anatomy, physics, math, chemistry, and computer science. Of course, new subjects are continually added to the program. Typically, the PASS program has between 30 to 40 leaders per year (S. Rogan, personal communication, February 13, 2006). Due to the Industrial Relations system in Australia, the wages of PASS leaders at

UOW would be very high compared with the pay provided to leaders in the United States (S. Rogan, personal communication, February 22, 2006). To offset the high cost of monetary compensation, UOW leaders receive credit for a course entitled Reflective Learning: Leadership & Peer Mentoring. This title reflects the importance placed upon leadership development and fostering strong relationships among students, faculty, and staff. Sally Rogan, PASS program manager, states: "It's a delight to work with the PASS peer leaders and see them grow and mature in their roles…"PASS is a win-win situation for everyone involved" (personal communication, March 1, 2006).

St. George's University, School of Medicine, Grenada, West Indies

Although most often associated with traditional colleges and universities, SI has also proven to be effective in medical school settings. St. George's University (SGU) – School of Medicine is located in St. Georges, Grenada, West Indies, which is an independent nation within the British Commonwealth. Well known for its unique and diverse culture, Grenada has a population of slightly more than 100,000 citizens. Grenada's residents are predominately of African descent, while some are of East Indian and European descent.

SGU was founded in 1976 and has faculty and students from 85 countries, thus, mirroring Grenada's rich cultural diversity. In 1993, SGU expanded its offerings to include graduate and undergraduate programs. In the years soon thereafter, programs in premedicine, international business, life sciences, liberal studies, medical sciences, and preveterinary medicine were launched. Contributors to SGU's health sciences training program include visiting medical professors from prestigious institutions such as Cornell, McGill University, Harvard, and London School of Tropical Health (St. George's University, n.d.).

SI was first employed in the spring of 2000 in the premedicine program, located within SGU's Department of Educational Services. Out of necessity, SGU's SI format differs from the traditional model in that upper-level students are not used as SI leaders. Instead, SI leaders are hired as part-time faculty employees and must have undergraduate degrees or significant experience in the sciences. As in the original model, SI leaders attend classes, have formal SI training, and meet with professors and supervisors on a weekly basis.

Currently, there are six courses supported by SI: general chemistry, molecular biology, microbiology, genetics, anatomy, and physiology. Although the majority of students enrolled in these courses are from the premedicine program, an increasing number of students from the life sciences and preveterinary programs also participate (P. Slinger, personal communication, February 10, 2005).

Additionally, the SI program has also taken the unique step of integrating SI strategies into SGU's more conventional tutoring or group review sessions. Approximately 120 of these groups, offered by upper-level students, meet each week. According to SI supervisor, Peter Slinger, "It is our intention to create an overarching atmosphere of active participation throughout all of our small-group activities" (personal communication, February 24, 2006). SI at SGU exemplifies the benefits that the program can offer to both students and the institutions they attend. SGU's premedicine program has earned much praise. Longitudinal data demonstrate that SGU's premedicine students who matriculate into the SGU medical school outperform students from other institutions (P. Slinger, personal communication, February 24, 2006).

SI at SGU is designed to promote academic success by helping students learn strategies that will improve their ability to integrate information from several different courses. Additionally, SI promotes the processing of detailed information and complex systems. Ultimately, the SI model enhances a future physician's ability to turn theory into practice. According to Slinger,

St. George's University has a strong tradition of assisting health professions' students to become more efficient, effective, and successful learners in the medical sciences. The SI program has assisted the university in spreading this philosophy to student learning in its other programs. (personal communication, February 24, 2006).

Nelson Mandela Metropolitan University, South Africa

Nelson Mandela Metropolitan University (NMMU) was created from the union of three prominent South African institutions: Port Elizabeth Technikon, the University of Port Elizabeth, and Vista University-Port Elizabeth campus. The emergence of NMMU reflects the government's encouragement of traditional universities fusing with technical institutions in order to create comprehensive educational systems capable of meeting the needs of a changing South Africa (Zerger, Clark-Unite, & Smith, 2006). Established in 2005, NMMU has more than 20,000 students and approximately 2,000 staff members and spans seven campuses. NMMU offers academic programs in the following faculties (or colleges): Arts, Business and Economic Sciences, Education, Engineering, the Built Environment and Information Technology, Health Sciences, Law, and Science.

SI was first piloted at the University of Port Elizabeth in 1993, and its emergence in South Africa coincided with the country's first democratic elections in 1994. During this period of change within a post-apartheid society, institutions of higher education initiated reform that promoted increased access for all citizens. With access came a growing number of underprepared and first-generation students (Zerger et al. 2006). Although SI is a renowned academic support model, it has also proven to be an effective tool for facilitating institutional change in a country that has experienced a great deal of societal change. SI creates a space that accommodates heterogeneous groups, in which students work together from diverse backgrounds and different levels of preparedness and are treated equally. SI is viewed as the catalyst in establishing a learning culture, creating a protected space for students where they can strengthen faith in their own abilities, ask critical questions, adapt to university life, and build empowering relationships while simultaneously taking responsibility for their own learning development. Cathy Clark-Unite, former Head of the SI national office at NMMU, emphasizes, "The program has played a critical role during the transformation period" (personal communication, March 6, 2006). While most academic support programs were phased out when the three universities merged to form NMMU, the SI program emerged with increased strength.

SI serves as NMMU's main mechanism for providing academic support. Currently, SI is used within 21 academic departments and includes 78 courses across several colleges. With more than 46 SI leaders and 90 SI sessions per week, the SI program has excellent attendance rates and is highly respected by campus administrators. Additionally, NMMU has collected solid quantitative data that consistently support the significant, positive relationship between SI attendance and academic performance. Ability, measured by matriculation (end of secondary school) results, and attendance at SI were correlated with university exam results. Ability was included in the analysis to determine whether the increase in academic performance was due to SI attendance or entering student characteristics. Attending SI contributed a positive and significant difference to the variance ($p < .05$; Clark-Unite & Smith, 2005).

SI's staying power is due to the many benefits the program provides. For example, because government support is based on student retention, SI has proven to be a cost-effective intervention for the university. Additionally, SI promotes positive social change within the student body (Zerger et al., 2006) because the SI sessions encourage peer interaction through the sharing of ideas and experiences (Martin & Wilcox, 1996). Additionally, this empowering atmosphere provides a safe forum for students to express their concerns to leaders who, in turn, can convey this feedback to faculty. SI proves to be an incredible mechanism in that "this feedback loop has given the students a voice" (Zerger et al., 2006, p. 67). At NMMU, SI has proven to be an effective academic support model and a powerful catalyst for positive educational and social change.

Lund University, Sweden

Sweden's largest research and higher education institution, Lund University has more than 42,000 students and 6,000 employees and has two major branches: Lund Institute of Technology and the Faculty of Humanities and Theology. As with the majority of Swedish universities, Lund University is managed by the government Ministry of Education and Science. Students do not pay tuition but pay a very low student union fee to attend university. Swedish culture promotes the basic principle that any student who needs financial help to attain an education should be able to receive student loans from the government. In fact, students who meet minimum academic standards typically qualify for some monetary assistance and grants that do not have to be repaid (Bryngfors & Barmen, 2003).

Several years ago, Sweden's government began a campaign to increase the number of Swedes earning university degrees. Since 1990, the number of students in higher education has increased by more than 50%, despite the fact that the total population of the country has grown by only about 5% in the same period. One consequence of this campaign is that higher numbers of underprepared students are now being admitted to Lund University. Despite the large numbers of underprepared students, the university still aims to retain approximately 75% of first-year students (Lund Institute of Technology, 1997). This is the same goal it had prior to the government's campaign. Approximately 50% of the government's funding for the university is based on enrollment, and the other 50% is based on retention demonstrated by "credits earned" (Bryngfors & Barmen, 2003). The challenge of retaining students was the impetus for implementing SI at Lund University (Wilcox, 1996).

SI is offered by the two major branches of Lund University. Lund Institute of Technology implemented an SI program in 1994, which has approximately 25 leaders and provides sessions in calculus, algebra, and chemistry. The Lund Institute of Technology has 18 programs (e.g., civil engineering, electrical engineering) at two campuses, and SI sessions are offered in seven of these programs. Involvement in the SI program is high, with 50% to 90% of students participating (L. Bryngfors, personal communication, February 26, 2006).

The second area in which SI is available is the faculty (or college) of humanities and theology, which offers SI in all the 16 departments (e.g., archeology and ancient history, East Asian languages, German, and philosophy). Piloted in the humanities in 2001, the SI program currently has 15 supervisors, each of whom works with up to nine leaders (85 leaders in total). About 35% of humanities students were active in SI, which Lund University defines as attending 20% of available sessions. While only 50% of non-SI students finished the term passing all their courses, well over 75% of SI students successfully did so (C. Gillis, personal communication, February 21, 2006).

The programs highlighted in this chapter differ from the traditional U.S. model in several ways: (a) leaders work in pairs, (b) students are enrolled in sections of SI, and (c) SI is a tool for facilitating institutional and social change, increasing the number of students attending university. However, the attainment of knowledge and helping students to be academically successful are common goals shared by all SI institutions.

Future Directions

For more than three decades, SI has supported students' academic pursuits and professional aspirations. It has expanded beyond its traditional boundaries through areas such as professional development, distance learning, and community education. While the effectiveness of SI has been proven across numerous disciplines (Burmeister et al., 1994; Kenney & Kallison, 1994; Lockie & Van Lanen, 1994; Martin & Hurley, 2005; Zerger, 1994) and with a variety of populations (Bidgood, 1994; Martin & Arendale, 1993; Martin, Blanc, & Arendale, 1996; Ramirez, 1997), there is still uncharted territory into which SI can expand. One adaptation that has already been implemented with promising success is SI in high schools. A few other possible innovations will be explored here.

Campus Innovations

The structure of the SI model has changed very little in 35 years. University campuses are dynamic institutions; however, they need to continually reexamine themselves to keep pace with the changing times. With advancements in technology and the ongoing development of new programs across college campuses, it is time to consider partnerships and adaptations that could enhance the SI experience, whether it is in traditional institutions of higher learning, or in professional schools supporting their students to pass standardized and licensing exams.

SI and learning communities. In recent years, the attention of administrators and faculty has turned toward the concept of learning communities. Learning communities involve the coordination of two or more courses into a single program of instruction and often include the opportunity for student members to live collectively, as well. Regardless of the residential arrangement of the program, research has shown that learning communities help students feel connected to and supported by the campus, which can lead to improved learning, retention, and academic achievement. Students benefit by learning to think critically, integrating content across the disciplines, and doing so in a collaborative environment.

As SI was developed to provide students the opportunity to interact as they engage with difficult course content, SI and learning communities seem like natural partners. The shared goals and objectives of SI and learning communities enable the two programs to easily complement and strengthen one another. Integrating SI into learning communities provides additional opportunities for students to interact on both an academic and social level, thus improving connections between students, enhancing group cohesiveness, and strengthening student involvement in both programs.

SI and teaching-learning centers. Teaching-learning centers are a relatively new resource for faculty members that have emerged at colleges and universities across the nation. Developed in response to our collective, continually improved understanding of student learning, teaching-learning centers provide encouragement, support, and instruction to faculty members to incorporate classroom strategies that encourage critical processing and understanding, not just rote memorization. These centers frequently offer faculty workshops and additional materials on how to enhance content delivery methods, implement interactive strategies, and ultimately, improve student learning. Teaching-learning centers could incorporate the proven, collaborative learning strategies that are the hallmarks of SI. The same tactics that SI uses to engage students in the learning process (e.g., wait-time, redirection, checking for understanding), as well as specific session strategies (e.g., concept mapping, matrices and diagrams, vocabulary exercises, problem-solving board work) would lend themselves to classroom use and could greatly improve classroom interaction and student outcomes.

Distance learning programs. With advancements in technology occurring at such a rapid pace, it is not surprising that the culture of higher education is being affected in many ways. Distance education (i.e., online courses) have changed the way instruction is delivered and that students learn. While it offers many benefits, including flexibility of time and location, virtual instruction poses challenges as well. A modified form of SI can offer students the interaction that is often the most significant deficiency in this 21st century form of education.

In online courses, as in traditional live classrooms, there are students who need help processing content. Effective SI sessions allow students to process information efficiently. Online versions of SI can accomplish the same goals (Painter, 2004). Students can come together virtually to discuss difficult content, contemplate questions, share strategies, and discuss complex concepts, just as they do in person during traditional SI sessions. Advantages of this format might include the same flexibility of time and place and a safer, more anonymous environment for students to share and ask questions. Potential disadvantages include technical problems, computer illiteracy, cost of implementation, and disorganization of sessions due to the lack of physical and temporal proximity of participants (Painter).

Community Applications

SI and the business sector. The corporate world realizes the importance of teamwork, sharing ideas, resolving conflict, and collectively processing what are often excruciatingly complex models, theorems, or strategies. The same fundamental tenets that define classroom SI could be applied to facilitating groups of lifelong learners working in virtually any type of business or commercial setting. Strategies that have proven invaluable to student learning could be easily transferred to the corporate arena. Similarly, the structure of video-based SI (see chapter 7) could be replicated for use in business and industry, allowing for dissemination of information across time or distance.

SI and social justice. SI is a mechanism for meaningful transformation, both for individuals and institutions. Its evolution into an international vehicle for change is a natural progression, as can be inferred from SI's successful implementation into various worldwide locations. SI can assist struggling populations facing a multitude of needs, particularly those found in developing countries.

By working with nonprofit relief and educational agencies around the world, it is possible that adaptations of SI and video-based SI programs could support critical educational efforts for all people. These programs could help initiate and reinforce what could be life-changing knowledge and awareness programs that combat difficulties such as abject poverty, insufficient health care, and/or underfunded or substandard educational systems.

Conclusion

Over the last three decades, SI has evolved from a fledgling program on a midwestern university campus to an international model that has been adopted on five continents, including the newest programs in Hong Kong and India. The expansion of SI has been remarkable, yet its evolution is far from over. Enriched by international collaboration, SI has established itself as a premier academic support program. SI continues to flourish and progress in response to the changing educational Zeitgeist, i.e., SI adapts to society's ever changing needs. But SI need not be confined by the conventional dictates of the academic milieu. Because of the model's versatility, with little effort, it can be customized to meet the requirements of nearly any situation. We are only just beginning to understand the possible applications and contributions SI has to offer.

Authors' Note

The authors would like to personally thank and formally acknowledge the invaluable contributions of the following SI colleagues in composing this chapter. They are tremendous assets to their students, their institutions, and the international SI community.

William Carey, University of Manchester - United Kingdom
Sally Rogan, University of Wollongong - Australia
Peter Slinger, St. George's University School of Medicine - Grenada, WestIndies
Cathy Clark-Unite, Nelson Mandela Metropolitan University - South Africa
Carole Gillis and Leif Bryngfors, Lund University - Sweden

Notes

[1]Data collected fall 2003 to spring 2004 on 33 courses, N = 6,109.
[2]Data collected spring 2002 to spring 2003 on five courses, N = 1,868.

References

Ashwin, P. (1994). The Supplemental Instruction leader experience, why supplemental is not teaching: A student's perspective. In C. R. Rust & J. Wallace (Eds.), *Helping students to learn from each other: Supplemental Instruction* (pp. 87-90). Birmingham, England: Staff and Educational Development Association.

Bidgood, P. (1994). The success of Supplemental Instruction: Statistical evidence. In C. Rust & J. Wallace (Eds.), *Helping students to learn from each other: Supplemental Instruction* (pp. 71-79). Birmingham, UK: Staff and Educational Development Association.

Bryngfors, L., & Barmen, G. (2003). The LTH program – A structured introductory process to improve first-year students' performance and learning. *NASPA Journal, 40*(4), 38-54.

Burmeister, S. L., Carter, J. M., Hockenberger, L. R., Kenney, P. A., McLaren, A., & Nice, D. (1994). Supplemental Instruction sessions in college algebra and calculus. In D. C. Martin & D. Arendale (Eds.), *Supplemental Instruction: Increasing achievement and retention* (pp. 53-61). San Francisco: Jossey-Bass.

Clark-Unite, C., & Smith, L. (2005). *NMMU SI funding report for ABE Bailey Trust Fund*. Unpublished report: NMMU, Port Elizabeth.

Coe, E. M., McDougall, A. O., & McKeown, N. B. (1999). Is peer-assisted learning of benefit to undergraduate chemists? *University Chemistry Education, 3*(2), 72-75.

Donelan, M. (1999, May). *SI leaders: The real winners*. Paper presented at the national conference on Supplemental Instruction, Kansas City, MO.

Fostier, M., Sheffield, L., & Speake, T. (2006, May). *Evaluation of the implementation of Peer Assisted Study Sessions (PASS) on a major scale for biosciences 1st year undergraduates at Manchester University (UK)*. Poster presented at the 4th International Conference on Supplemental Instruction, Malmö, Sweden.

Garside, J., Embury, S., & Carey, W. (2006, May). *Changing the student, changing the culture*. Paper presented at the 4th International Conference on Supplemental Instruction, Malmö, Sweden.

Kenney, P. A., & Kallison, Jr., J. M. (1994). Research studies on the effectiveness of Supplemental Instruction in mathematics. In D. C. Martin & D. Arendale (Eds.), *Supplemental Instruction: Increasing achievement and retention* (pp.75-82). San Francisco: Jossey-Bass.

Lockie, N. M., & Van Lanen, R. J. (1994). Supplemental Instruction for college chemistry courses. In D. C. Martin & D. Arendale (Eds.), *Supplemental Instruction: Increasing achievement and retention* (pp. 63-74). San Francisco: Jossey-Bass, 1994.

Lund Institute of Technology. (1997). (In Swedish). *The goal of a successful educational program*. Statements of the program boards of education. Report on education quality, Q 1997:2, LTH.

Martin, D. C., & Arendale, D. (1993). Supplemental Instruction in the first college year. In D. C. Martin & D. Arendale (Eds.), *Supplemental Instruction: Improving first-year student success in high-risk courses* (Monograph No. 7, pp. 11-18). Columbia, SC: National Resource Center for The Freshman Year Experience, University of South Carolina.

Martin, D. C., & Blanc, R. (1994). Supplemental Instruction: An organic model in transition, the view of SI's initiator. In C. Rust & J. Wallace (Eds.), *Helping students to learn from each other: Supplemental Instruction* (pp. 91-94). Birmingham, England: Staff and Educational Development Association.

Martin, D. C., Blanc, R. A., & Arendale, D. (1996). Supplemental Instruction: Supporting the classroom experience. In J. N. Hankin (Ed.), *The community college: Opportunity and access for America's first-year Students* (Monograph No. 19, pp. 123-133). Columbia, SC: National Resource Center for The Freshman Year Experience and Students in Transition, University of South Carolina.

Martin, D. C., & Hurley, M. (2005). Supplemental Instruction. In M. L. Upcraft, J. N. Gardner, & B. O. Barefoot (Eds.), *Challenging and supporting the first-year student: A handbook for improving the first year of college* (pp. 308-319). San Francisco: Jossey-Bass.

Martin, D. C., & Wilcox, F. K. (1996). Supplemental Instruction: Helping students to help each other. In G. Wisker (Ed.), *Enabling student learning: Systems and strategies* (pp. 97-101). London: Staff and Educational Development Association, Kogan Page.

Painter, S. L. (2004, June). *Online SI: To boldly go where no SI has gone before.* Presentation at the 3rd International Conference on Supplemental Instruction, Boston, MA.

Ramirez, G. (1997). Supplemental Instruction: The long-term impact. *Journal of Developmental Education, 21*(1), 2-9.

St. George University. (n.d.). History. Retrieved March 11, 2008 from http://www.sgu.edu/website/sguwebsite.nsf/about-sgu/sgu-history.html

Stone, M. E., Jacobs, G., & Hayes, H. (2006). Supplemental Instruction (SI): Student perspectives in the 21st century. In D. B. Lundell, J. L. Higbee, I. M., Duranczyk, & E. Goff (Eds.), *Student standpoints about access program in higher education* (pp. 129-141). Minneapolis, MN: Center for Research on Developmental Education and Urban Literacy, General College, University of Minnesota.

University of Manchester. (n.d.a). *History and origins.* Retrieved February 17, 2005, from http://www.manchester.ac.uk/aboutus/facts/history/

University of Manchester. (n.d.b). *Students and staff.* Retrieved February 17, 2005, from http://www.manchester.ac.uk/aboutus/facts/statistics/studentsandstaff/

University of Wollogong (UOW). (2003-2004). [Unpublished raw data].

University of Wollogong (UOW). (2002-2003). [Unpublished raw data].

Wallace, J. (1992). Students helping students to learn. *The New Academic, 1*(2), 8-9.

Wilcox, F. K. (1996, Summer). Supplemental Instruction in Sweden: An interview with Marita Bruzell-Nilsson and Leif Bryngfors. *Supplemental Instruction Update*, 1-3.

Zerger, S. (1994). Supplemental Instruction in the content areas: Humanities. In D. C. Martin & D. Arendale (Eds.), *Supplemental Instruction: Increasing achievement and retention* (pp. 41-52). San Francisco: Jossey-Bass.

Zerger, S. (2005). *Progress report on certification process for Supplemental Instruction / peer-assisted study sessions: University of Wollongong.* Unpublished report: UMKC, Kansas City, MO.

Zerger, S., Clark-Unite, C., & Smith, L. (2006). How Supplemental Instruction (SI) benefits faculty, administration, and institutions. In M. E. Stone & G. Jacobs (Eds.), *New visions for Supplemental Instruction (SI): SI for the 21st century* (pp. 63-72). San Francisco: Jossey-Bass.

Chapter 9

Epilogue: Concluding the First 35 Years

Amelia McDaniel

For many students, college is merely an experience that must be endured in order to find a better job and earn a higher wage. Their instructors are often intimidating; they constantly are being asked to perform tasks they do not know how to do; and they cannot appreciate why certain courses or degree programs are organized as they are. One way students choose to manage this disjunction is by relying on memorization rather than understanding. While this will not work in every situation, often memorization will carry a student through enough courses to earn an undergraduate degree. SI is an alternative coping mechanism for many of these students. Students who are better prepared for college-level coursework understand the value of studying with their classmates, especially with someone who has taken the course before, and they take advantage of it for that reason. Not necessarily high-risk or low-performing, students who attend SI are both novice learners who have not mastered expert problem-solving strategies and accomplished students who want to take advantage of every opportunity that is offered to them.

SI is one of the only college-level academic support programs that teaches students transferable study strategies, and it does this by building a bridge between what students are motivated to do—earn high grades—and what they need to do so—have exposure to effective learning strategies. Rather than offering study skills education in isolation, SI attaches to an historically difficult course and offers students an opportunity to work together, guided by a peer who knows the course, material, and instructor.

Thirty-five years of research on SI has found that the collaboration that takes place in SI sessions continues to help students earn higher grades, and that is encouraging because the number of students entering college increases every year (NCES, 2005). As SI programs expand to meet the demands of increasing enrollment, program administrators need to be mindful of how important it is to maintain high standards in training and observation of leaders. Because SI leaders are often some of the best students on campus, it is easy for supervisors to believe they can be trusted and need little monitoring. Even the strongest leaders, however, need consistent guidance and support from their supervisors. By being conscientious in training and supervising leaders, we can ensure that students continue to have positive experiences in SI sessions, wherever they are in the world.

In the last 35 years, SI has expanded from near the geographic center of the United States to the far reaches of the globe. Programs in Canada, Mexico, Sweden, the United Kingdom, South Africa, Australia, Hong Kong, and Grenada have added their unique flavor to the SI formula. All of these permutations of SI have helped us better understand how students learn. The exciting part of this is that SI is adaptable enough to be applied successfully in such diverse environments, yet the basics that make SI unique have held true: Collaboration is the key.

Many of the basic learning strategies that SI has relied on for decades to encourage collaboration are still favorites of leaders and students. The informal quiz and note review, for example, are generic strategies that are used with great success across disciplines; however, recent research in teaching and learning suggests that expert learners use discipline-specific strategies, while novice learners do not. This does not imply that generic learning strategies have no place in SI, but it does suggest that students may benefit from the incorporation of more discipline-specific strategies into SI sessions. Supervisors have an opportunity and an obligation to begin developing additional strategies to share with leaders.

Another area of SI that deserves additional attention from supervisors is that of the learning theory that gave birth to SI. From cognitivism to cooperative learning, theory helps us support and adapt our practice. Understanding why something works helps one know how to adjust it, when necessary, without omitting or altering essential characteristics. Leaders will also benefit from lessons in learning theory; it makes an excellent topic for ongoing training sessions throughout the semester.

The same learning theory that supports the goals and methods of SI also validates Video-Based Supplemental Instruction (VSI). A program designed specifically for underprepared students, VSI integrates study strategies directly into the classroom. With trained facilitators who control the pace of the recorded lecture, VSI gives students more time on task and more guidance than a traditional lecture section. Its success in the early 1990s continues today. VSI has become a part of secondary education in rural Missouri where college-level courses are not otherwise available to students in high schools. VSI also provides similar opportunities to high school students in Sweden, while in South Africa, VSI is being used to increase access to higher education for students previously oppressed by apartheid.

Throughout this monograph, practitioners from the International Center for SI have shared their expert opinions about how SI and VSI work. Their intention is to leave readers with a better understanding of SI and VSI programs—how we know they work, how to implement them, how to underpin their practice with sound learning theory, how to market them, how to train staff, and, most importantly, how to maintain a professional enthusiasm for academic support programs that have helped millions of students find success. Without the continued work of practitioners whose applications of SI and VSI have informed our understanding of student success in a variety of contexts, this program would not continue to be adopted.

As SI moves into its next 35 years, practitioners can expect the program to grow not just in numbers, but in depth. Research in SI and VSI will continue to demonstrate their positive effect on student grades, but assessment of these efforts will need to examine less obvious outcomes. The ways in which SI benefits leaders, influences instructor pedagogy, impacts course evaluations, and arms students with transferable study skills should be examined and elucidated. Training of SI leaders and VSI facilitators can become an academic endeavor, and many leaders and mentors deserve course credit for their work in the SI program. Supervisors will find they need to continue to adapt and develop learning strategies to fit the growing need for new approaches to learning. And SI will continue to spread throughout the seven continents. What Deanna Martin started as a graduate student in 1973 will continue to be carried on by thousands of practitioners and appreciated by millions of students. SI is here to stay.

References

National Center for Education Statistics (NCES). (2005). *Postsecondary institutions in the United States: Fall 2003 and other awards conferred: 2002-03.* Washington, DC: U.S. Department of Education. Retrieved April 1, 2008, from http://nces.ed.gov/pubsearch/pubsinfo.asp?pubid=2005154

Appendix A

Glossary of Terms

Advanced Organizer: A learning strategy that a facilitator uses to help students connect new information and concepts to existing knowledge. They may be short sets of verbal or visual information presented before learning content or a brief introduction to the way that information is going to be structured or presented.

Boardwork Model: A learning strategy in which the board is used as a template for problem solving. The students are asked to list prerequisite information needed to solve a problem (e.g., formulas), record the mathematical steps of the solution, record the steps of the solution in narrative form, and construct a similar problem.

Concept Map: A webbed diagram used for exploring knowledge, brainstorming ideas, and organizing large amounts of material.

Dependency Cycle: Refers to pedagogical methods that rely on the learner remaining passive. The learner, because he or she does not take an active role in the process, always feels dependent on a source of knowledge such as the instructor, a text, or a tutor.

DFW Rate: The rate of Ds, Fs, and withdrawals earned by students in a given course or cohort.

Divide-and-Conquer Activities: A learning strategy in which the facilitator breaks up a large amount of material (usually a reading) into smaller segments, then assigns each segment to a student or group. The students study their portion and present a condensed version to the whole group.

Flowcharts and Diagrams: Visual models that allow students to organize information in a way that is meaningful to them.

Focus on Student Control: A phrase used in Video-Supplemental Instruction (VSI) to refer to the student's ability to direct the flow of information and the pace of learning during the VSI course meeting as opposed to a traditional lecture.

Incomplete Outline: A traditional outline where material is organized hierarchically and some levels are left blank for students to complete.

Informal Quiz: A learning strategy in which the facilitator asks students to write down their answers to questions given orally. The questions are designed to solicit short written answers and to stimulate the broad discussion which follows.

Jigsaws: A learning strategy in which a large group is divided into smaller groups, and each small group is given a specific task to perform (e.g., solve a problem, compile information for a history identification, write a simple program). Once the small groups have had time to work on their task, the large group reassembles to share the information.

Managed Study Time: A phrase used in VSI to refer to the extended length of VSI courses as compared to traditional lecture courses. Students are presented with content as well as guided study time in the course meeting.

Matrix: An organizational chart with columns and rows used to compare and contrast two or more subjects.

Metacognition: Thinking about thinking in general or reasoning about one's own thinking.

Note Review: A learning strategy in which students read through their notes, taking turns from subject to subject. While one student is reading, other students are encouraged to add to the discussion by providing missing information and questioning the content of his or her notes. Frequently used at the beginning of the semester.

One-Minute Paper: A learning strategy in which students are asked to write for one minute on a question or topic given by the leader. Helpful for refocusing, opening, or closing the session.

Paired Problem Solving: See Think Aloud.

P.A.L.: Peer-Assisted Learning, an alternative name for SI that is used in the United Kingdom.

P.A.S.S.: Peer-Assisted Study Sessions, an alternative name for SI that is used in Australia.

Polish: A strategy used in VSI to refer to an extension of the review process. Students polish their skills by reorganizing information, writing practice essays, predicting and formulating practice test questions, and testing one another.

Postexam Survey: A self-test for students in which they score themselves in areas necessary to do well on a specific exam (e.g., attended every lecture, took clear notes, read them again later and understood them, read and understood assigned texts, attended SI).

Preview: A strategy used in VSI to refer to the time students spend preparing for the presentation of new material. A facilitator uses preview to assess students' prior knowledge of a subject, discuss unfamiliar vocabulary, and cover the main ideas of the lecture. Preview activities might include defining vocabulary words from the lecture, discussing questions from the text in small groups, or brainstorming to determine prior knowledge.

Process: A term used in VSI to refer to the time when the facilitator stops the tape and allows the students to sort out or practice the material already presented.

Question Group Protocols: A learning strategy in which the facilitator asks students to work carefully through the foils, or possible answers, in a multiple-choice question, explaining why they are the correct answer or why they are not the correct answer but might be mistaken as such.

Reciprocal Questioning: Reciprocal questioning is an alternating question and answer process that aids students in acquiring a deeper understanding of content (e.g., an assigned reading or material for an exam review). The leader allows the students to ask questions of him/her first, and then the leader asks questions of the students. This procedure improves students' questioning and reasoning strategies, as well as their reading comprehension.

Review: A term used in VSI to refer to the process of re-examining course material after it has been previewed, presented, and processed. Reviews should occur during each course meeting.

Sequencing: A learning strategy in which the facilitator scrambles material and asks students to put it in the correct order (e.g., sequence of steps in solving a math problem or in a biological cycle).

SI Leader: A student with excellent interpersonal skills who has taken a course before and earned a high grade and is hired to attend the course lecture, model good student behavior, and facilitate group study sessions for the course.

SI Mentor: An experienced SI leader who receives additional training in the philosophy behind the SI model and the practice of observing sessions and debriefing with SI leaders. Mentors assist SI supervisors in running the SI program.

SI Supervisor: An individual who runs an SI program and supervises SI leaders.

Think Aloud: An established research technique used to understand how people think and learn. It requires students to verbalize (usually to a partner) what they are thinking about as they read a passage or as they solve a problem. The vocalization should include all thoughts, decisions, analyses, and conclusions. This procedure is often called *Paired Problem Solving* when the student is solving a problem.

Think-Pair-Share: A learning strategy in which students are instructed to (a) think about a question individually, (b) pair up to discuss their ideas, and (c) come together as one group to share and compare answers.

Timeline: A horizontal line that represents the continuum of time. Important events are inserted relative to each other, creating points on the line. Each point that denotes an event should be marked with the date, a brief description of the event, and significant person(s) involved.

Time to Think: A phrase used in VSI to refer to the time when a lecture tape is stopped and students are allowed time to process material that has been presented.

Unsuccessful Enrollment: Any final course assessment that is low enough to prevent a student from progressing in their degree program. This includes a withdrawal, withdrawal failing, and a grade of C through a D-, depending on the requirements of the program.

Vocabulary Development: A learning strategy in which the facilitator provides students with a list of important terms at differing levels of specificity (can also use formulas or symbols for problem-solving material) and asks them to (a) group them in a way that is meaningful to them and (b) define one or two selected terms. The purpose is to encourage students to organize information to learn it faster and to prompt discussion.

Wait-Time (1): The amount of time a facilitator waits between asking a question and restating, rewording, or asking another question.

Wait-Time (2): The amount of time that passes between a response to a question and another utterance from the facilitator or a student.

Appendix B

Selected Annotated Bibliography for Supplemental Instruction

David R. Arendale

The Supplemental Instruction (SI) literature encompasses the largest number of scholarly publications and research studies in the field of postsecondary peer cooperative learning programs. The following bibliography represents only a sample of the more than 500 publications and research studies that have been conducted on SI in the United States and abroad and reflect the diverse academic disciplines, countries, and approaches. The works included here as well as those referenced throughout this monograph should be regarded as representative of the core body of research on SI. A complete SI bibliography with full annotations is available at http://www.tc.umn.edu/~arend011/Peerbib03.pdf

Arendale, D. (2001). Effect of administrative placement and fidelity of implementation of the model of effectiveness of Supplemental Instruction programs [Dissertation, University of Missouri – Kansas City, 2000]. *Dissertation Abstracts International, 62*, 93.

The entire known population of 735 SI programs within the United States was selected for study. There were statistically significant positive correlations with three of the four program activity constructs (SI Supervisor Involvement, SI Leader Involvement, and SI Leader training) and the effectiveness of the program regarding improved student outcomes and higher satisfaction ratings by the campus administrators who supervised the program. Implications from this research include identification of key activities within the program that should be observed to maximize program effectiveness for the institution and participating students.

Arendale, D. (2002). History of Supplemental Instruction: Mainstreaming of developmental education. In D. B. Lundell & J. L. Higbee (Eds.), *Histories of developmental education* (pp. 15-27). Minneapolis, MN: Center for Research on Developmental Education and Urban Literacy, General College, University of Minnesota.

This history of developmental education provides a context for creation of Supplemental Instruction to meet immediate needs at the institution due to a high attrition rate among students enrolled in professional schools. The national, and eventual international, dissemination of the SI model was due to its meeting similar needs at other institutions as well.

Arendale, D. (1995). Self-assessment for adjunct instructional programs. In S. Clark-Thayer (Ed.), *NADE self-evaluation guides: Models for assessing learning assistance/developmental education programs* (pp. 49-87). Clearwater, FL: H&H Publishing.

This chapter provides a framework for evaluating a campus SI program: mission, goals, and objectives; program activities; program administration; human resources; facilities; value system; awareness of individual differences; and program evaluation. Adjunct instructional programs (AIPs) are defined as group collaborative learning assistance that accompanies a specific targeted course to serve as a supplement for that course.

Ashwin, P. (2002). Implementing peer learning across organisations: The development of a model. *Mentoring & Tutoring, 10*(3), 221-231.

This article describes different ways to implement peer learning programs at institutions in the United Kingdom. A deeper understanding of organizational change can help guide administrators as they implement new programs. A version of SI using Lewin's (1952) theory of change has been contextualized for the British postsecondary education system.

Blanc, R. A., DeBuhr, L., & Martin, D. C. (1983). Breaking the attrition cycle: The effects of Supplemental Instruction on undergraduate performance and attrition. *Journal of Higher Education, 54*(1), 80-89.

This article concerns an evaluation of the SI program at the University of Missouri – Kansas City. The research study looked at the academic performance of 746 students enrolled in seven arts and sciences courses during spring 1980. A variety of research studies were completed using data gathered from this and subsequent academic terms. This article was the first one published outside of the field of developmental education to gain national attention concerning the SI model.

Bowles, T. J., & Jones, J. (2003). An analysis of the effectiveness of Supplemental Instruction: The problem of selection bias and limited dependent variables. *Journal of College Student Retention, 5*(2), 235-243.

This article moves beyond the usual reliance on single equation regression models to evaluate SI and employs a simultaneous equation, limited dependent variable evaluation model. Results of the research study at Utah State University at Logan suggest that students with below average academic ability are more likely to attend SI and that common measures of student ability included in single equation models fail to adequately control for this characteristic. The authors suggest that the older evaluation models have underestimated the effectiveness of SI.

Bridgham, R. G., & Scarborough, S. (1992). Effects of Supplemental Instruction in selected medical school courses. *Academic Medicine: Journal of the Association of American Medical Colleges, 67*(10), 569-571.

This article describes the use of SI in the College of Human Medicine of Michigan State University with courses in biochemistry, physiology, pharmacology, genetics, gross anatomy, and histology. The authors suggest about 20 specific activities for SI sessions. In general, SI participants earned higher mean final course grades. The authors mentioned that the success of the SI program has encouraged the college to maintain an admissions policy that enrolls a more diverse student population.

Bryngfors, L., & Barmen, G. (2003). The LTH Program—A structured introductory process to improve first-year students' performance and learning. *NASPA Journal, 40*(4), 38-54.

This article focuses on a comprehensive approach to student persistence at the Lund Institute of Technology in Sweden. The explorations led to the development of the LTH (*Swedish abbreviation for Lund Institute of Technology*) program, which combines an orientation process with a support system to help new students in their transition from secondary school to university studies. SI is an essential component of the program.

Burmeister, S. L., Kenney, P. A., & Nice, D. L. (1996). Analysis of effectiveness of Supplemental Instruction sessions for college algebra, calculus, and statistics. In J. J. Kaput, A. H. Schoenfeld, & E. Dubinsky (Eds.), *Research in collegiate mathematics education II* (pp. 145-154). Providence, RI: American Mathematical Association and Mathematical Association of America.

After an overview of the SI model, this article focuses on a research study concerning the effectiveness of SI for 11,252 students enrolled in 177 courses in college algebra, calculus, and statistics from 45 different institutions. In comparison with non-SI participants, SI participants earned higher mean final course grades and experienced lower rates of withdrawals: algebra (2.21 vs. 1.98); calculus (2.28 vs. 1.83); and statistics (2.49 vs. 2.32). These represent mean final course grades on a 4.0 scale.

Bushway, S. D., & Flower, S. M. (2002). Helping criminal justice students learn statistics: A quasi-experimental evaluation of learning assistance. *Journal of Criminal Justice Education, 13*(1), 35-57.

This article describes a quasi-experimental study of the use of SI in a statistics course taken by students enrolled in criminal justice and criminology at a large public university. Three other modifications were made in the class: (a) participation in SI was mandatory for at-risk students and voluntary for all others in the class; (b) web-based quizzes were offered; and (c) lecture class attendance was mandatory for at-risk students. The intent of the online quizzes was to increase reading of the textbook. SI and the quizzes contributed to increased success of students while the mandatory attendance did not have an apparent effect.

Capstick, S., & Fleming, H. (2002). Peer assisted learning in an undergraduate hospitality course: Second-year students supporting first-year students in group learning. *Journal of Hospitality, Leisure, Sport, and Tourism Education, 1*(1), 69-75.

This article describes the use of Peer Assisted Learning (PAL) in the Management Foundation Course within the School of Services Industries at Bournemouth University (United Kingdom). The article provides an overview of the PAL program and how it has been adapted from the SI model for use within the UK education system.

Clulow, V. G. (1998). *Supporting student learning in high-risk university subjects and the interrelationship to effective subject teaching: An analysis of a peer tutoring experience.* Unpublished doctoral dissertation, University of Melbourne, Parkville, Victoria, Australia. Retrieved July 1, 2004, from http://adt1.lib.unimelb.edu.au/adt-root/public/adt-VU2002.0003/

This dissertation is concerned with the detailed accounts of 21 students who participated with SI in a Statistics for Marketers course. SI was found to be significant for improving student involvement in the course that resulted in higher academic outcomes for the students. Students found that SI enabled learning from a subject "champion," symmetry in the teaching/learning communication, an effective use of learning time, and the opportunity to work in small groups.

Coe, E. M., McDougall, A. O., & McKeown, N. B. (1999). Is peer assisted learning of benefit to undergraduate chemists? *University Chemistry Education, 3*(2), 72-75.

Peer Assisted Study Sessions (PASS), based on Supplemental Instruction (SI), was implemented at the University of Manchester (UK) Chemistry Department in 1995 for first-year courses. About half of students enrolled in the classes where PASS is offered participate in the program. The drop-out rate was reduced by half after the introduction of PASS (from 20% to 10%). PASS Leaders also reported advantages for their participation, including improved communication skills.

Congos, D. H. (2001-2002). How Supplemental Instruction (SI) generates revenue for colleges and universities. *Journal of College Student Retention: Research, Theory, & Practice, 3*(3), 301-309.

The author shows how SI can create retained tuition revenue far beyond the costs of an SI program in both state-supported and private colleges and universities and notes that SI reduces recruiting costs and retains incoming tuition dollars for longer time periods, supplements the quality of the educational experience, and has the potential to affect an institution's fundraising efforts.

Donelan, M., & Kay, P. (1998). Supplemental Instruction: Students helping students' learning at University College London (UCL) and University of Central Lancashire (UCLAN). *The International Journal of Legal Education, 32*(3), 287-299.

The SI program is used to meet the needs of first-year students in their academic and personal development within the law faculties of the University College London (UCL) and the University of Central Lancashire (UCLAN). The United Kingdom expansion of the SI model has helped develop, more holistically, the cognitive and affective aspects of learning for both SI participants and SI leaders. Benefits cited by the SI leaders included an opportunity to help others; developed communication, presentation, and leadership skills; and increased knowledge of the academic content of the course.

Eastmond, J. N. (1997). Five academic development programs in the Eastern Cape Province: Reactions of an American academic in South Africa. *Educational Technology Research & Development, 45*(3), 129-134.

This article describes the academic development programs at four tertiary institutions in South Africa (University of Port Elizabeth, Port Elizabeth Technikon, Rhodes University, and the University of Ft. Hare) as well as the development of a fifth new program at Border Technikon. Topics include cross-cultural differences, interviews, SI that combined staff development and student academic development, integration of media support, and program development.

Etter, E. R., Burmeister, S. L., & Elder, R. J. (2000). Improving student performance and retention via Supplemental Instruction. *Journal of Accounting Education, 18*, 355-368.

This study reports on student performance and failure and withdrawal rates for 9,053 students enrolled in 132 Principles of Accounting classes from 21 four-year colleges and universities that have adopted the SI program. The overall SI participation rate was 26.8%. SI participants were found to have statistically significant higher average course grades (2.44 vs. 2.12, on a 4.0 scale), lower failure rates (5.9% vs. 15.3%), and lower withdrawal rates (10.6% vs. 19.8%) than nonparticipants enrolled in the target courses.

Feinn, R. (2004). Effectiveness of Supplemental Instruction for developmental math in a university setting. *Dissertation Abstracts International, 65*(02), 410.

This dissertation explored the utility of SI at a public university in New England with an elementary algebra course. Students who participated in SI sessions facilitated by instructors had higher final course grades than groups that were led by peer student leaders.

Forester, J. P., Thomas, P. P., & McWhorter, D. L. (2004). Effects of four Supplemental Instruction programs on students' learning of gross anatomy. *Clinical Anatomy, 17*(4), 322-327.

This article evaluated the effectiveness of SI when adapted for use through four interventions: (a) second-year medical student teaching assistant program, (b) directed study program, (c) weekly instructor laboratory reviews, and (d) a web-based anatomy program. In each case, participants in the adapted SI programs earned higher grades and self-reported higher levels of satisfaction when compared with nonparticipants.

Gattis, K. W. (2002). Responding to self-selection bias in assessments of academic support programs: A motivational control study of Supplemental Instruction. *The Learning Assistance Review, 7*(2), 26-36.

A motivational control study of students participating in SI sessions in college chemistry at North Carolina State University showed that participants benefit from SI sessions to an extent that cannot be explained by their higher levels of motivation. Motivation is shown to be an important factor in grade performance whether students use SI or not. Actual SI attendance is shown to provide additional grade benefits.

Hafer, G. R. (2001). Supplemental Instruction in freshman composition. *Journal of Developmental Education, 24*(3), 30-32, 34, 36-37.

In the past, SI has been underused in first-year composition courses particularly because of misperceptions regarding the nature of composition and the notion that the writing laboratory provides the only needed assistance programs. This article examines those assumptions and explores how success is measured in the composition classroom. It argues that the goals and method of first-year composition and SI are complementary.

Hodges, R., Dochen, C. W., & Joy, D. (2001). Increasing students' success: When Supplemental Instruction becomes mandatory. *Journal of College Reading and Learning, 31*(2), 143-156.

The study found that students in both mandated and voluntary SI groups in a high risk, required, first-year, writing-intensive United States history course earned significantly higher course grades and semester grade point averages than students in the non-SI group.

Hurley, K. F., McKay, D. W., Scot, T. M., & James, B. M. (2003). The Supplemental Instruction project: Peer-devised and delivered tutorials. *Medical Teacher, 25*(4), 404-407.

The study examined the effectiveness of Supplemental Instruction Program (SIP) with first-year undergraduate medical students at Memorial University of Newfoundland in the Integrated Study of Disease I course during 1998 and 2000. The SIP program is based on the Medical Scholars Program developed at the University of Southern California, which is an adaptation of SI. Both qualitative and quantitative data collection methods were employed to evaluate the program.

Hurley, M. A. (2000). Video-based Supplemental Instruction (VSI): An interactive delivery system that facilitates student learning [Dissertation, University of Missouri – Kansas City, 1999]. *Dissertation Abstracts International, 61*(04), 1317.

The study focuses on the cognitive and affective results of a small-group learning model called VSI. VSI students learned a variety of strategies, which provided them with the academic tools to be successful on their history exams in that class. VSI students developed a greater sense of self-efficacy in the class. Students developed greater personal confidence because of the VSI experience.

Jarvi, S. W. (1998). A quantitative and qualitative examination of Supplemental Instruction and its relationship to student performance (collaborative learning, academic support) (Dissertation, University of Connecticut, 1998). *Dissertation Abstracts International, 59*(05), 1484A.

Quantitative and qualitative methodologies were employed in this study. The sample for the quantitative component included 2,295 cases of students' completing 1 of 12 introductory level biology or chemistry courses in which SI was offered at a large research university in New England. Analyses of data found that in 7 of 12 classes involved, level of participation in SI explained a significant additional amount of variation in exam scores with accompanying large effect sizes. Qualitative findings revealed core categories related to why students attend SI.

Kochenour, E. O., Jolley, D. S., Kaup, J. G., Patrick, D. L., Roach, K. D., & Wenzler, L. A. (1997). Supplemental Instruction: An effective component of student affairs programming. *Journal of College Student Development, 38*(6), 577-586.

The effectiveness of SI was examined using 11,000 participants enrolled in eight courses at the University of Utah, a large research university. Correlational analyses and analysis of covariance support the hypothesis that SI is an effective program. Though students of various previous levels of academic achievement attended SI in similar patterns, research suggests that SI sessions had the most impact on students with lower previous grade point averages.

Lundeberg, M. A., & Moch, S. D. (1995). Influence of social interaction on cognition: Connected learning in science. *Journal of Higher Education, 66*(3), 312-335.

This article explores the use of SI for increasing the academic success of women in science. A research study of nursing students at the University of Wisconsin (River Falls) was conducted to test this idea. Qualitative research studies of the SI sessions suggested the following themes: spirit of cooperation, a circle of community, a shift of power to the SI participants, and risk-taking behavior (acknowledge uncertainty, experiment with new ideas without fear of lower grades or punishment).

Martin, D. C. (1980). Learning centers in professional schools. In K. V. Lauridsen (Ed.), *Examining the scope of learning centers* (pp. 69-79). San Francisco: Jossey-Bass.

This chapter describes the role of academic assistance for students in professional schools. The use of SI for medical students is described. Several research studies suggest that SI contributes to higher academic achievement and the rate of Ds, Fs, and course withdrawals have been reduced by 20%. Data suggest that there is a transfer effect of SI: Students who take advantage of SI to maintain their GPA lead over nonparticipating students during the following academic term in the second course in the same sequence.

Martin, D. C., Blanc, R. A., & Arendale, D. (1994). Mentorship in the classroom: Making the implicit explicit. *Teaching Excellence, 6*(1), 1-2.

Based upon experiences gained through the SI program, the authors make a number of suggestions on how faculty members can use SI strategies in their classes.

Martin, D. C., & Hurley, M. (2005). Supplemental Instruction. In M. L. Upcraft, J. N. Gardner, & B. O. Barefoot (Eds.), *Challenging & supporting the first-year student: A handbook for improving the first year of college* (pp. 308-319). San Francisco: Jossey-Bass.

This chapter provides an overview of SI. After providing guiding principles of SI, evidence of effectiveness is cited from the University of Missouri – Kansas City and several other representative institutions. Two adaptations of the SI model are cited: Video-based SI and the Advanced Preparation Program. The chapter closes with recommendations for increasing the effectiveness of SI.

Mason, D., & Verdel, E. (2001). Gateway to success for at-risk students in a large-group introductory chemistry class. *Journal of Chemical Education, 78*(2), 252-255.

This study examined students enrolled at The University of Texas at San Antonio regarding the impact of a special program for at-risk students enrolled in a chemistry course with no laboratory component. SI was one part of this special program. The study was carefully controlled regarding the possible impact of variables. At-risk students were enrolled in both a large lecture class and a small one.

Maxwell, W. E. (1998). Supplemental Instruction, learning communities, and studying together. *Community College Review, 26*(2), 1-18.

This study was designed to investigate the extent to which peer relations increased among students who participated in a modified program of SI at a large community college in California. SI was modified by using instructors from the regular courses and, to a lesser extent, by financial aid counselors. Research suggests that the SI workshops promoted the growth of student study networks.

McGee, J. V. (2005). *Cognitive, demographic, and motivational factors as indicators of help-seeking in Supplemental Instruction.* Unpublished doctoral dissertation, Texas A & M University, College Station, TX. Retrieved November 24, 2006, from https://txspace.tamu.edu/bitstream/1969.1/2325/1/etd-tamu-2005A-EDAD-McGee.pdf

The purpose of this study was to determine how cognitive, demographic, and motivational factors can be used to understand help-seeking behavior in college students. Extrinsic motivation, organization, academic self-efficacy, control beliefs, help-seeking, and peer learning were the motivational scales that best predicted SI engagement. Students who were highly engaged in SI had significantly higher mean final course grades than either nonparticipants or low-engagement students even controlling for differences in SAT scores, cumulative grade point average, and motivation.

Murray, M. H. (1997). Students, learning resources: An inseparable triad. *Australian Journal of Engineering Education, 7*(2), 129-139

This paper describes the use of SI at the School of Engineering, Queensland University of Technology (Australia) with two first-year engineering courses. SI is compared with the traditional, lecture-centered model of learning. The introductory engineering courses were reorganized to integrate SI into the learning delivery system. Based on the seven-point grading scale employed in Australian education (1 = low; 7 = high), the academic performance of students with SI was raised to 4.3 from the previous level of 3.0 before the introduction of the SI model.

Phelps, J. M. (2005). *Supplemental Instruction in a community college developmental mathematics curriculum: A phenomenological study of learning experiences.* Unpublished doctoral dissertation, University of Central Florida, Orlando, FL.

This research study used a phenomenological approach at a community college to identify factors that motivated students' attendance and subsequent learning experiences in SI sessions that supported developmental mathematics courses. Interviews were held with both SI participants and the SI leaders. Additional data were gathered through a Multiple Intelligence Inventory. The data suggested eight themes of motivation for students participating in the voluntary SI sessions and nine themes characterized the types of learning experiences that occurred in the SI session. SI was found to be a significant factor in academic achievement in the developmental mathematics courses.

Rust, C., & Wallace, J. (Eds.). (1994). *Helping students to learn from each other: Supplemental Instruction.* Birmingham, England: Staff and Educational Development Association.

This monograph provides a comprehensive review of SI in the United Kingdom: overview of SI, and the introduction of SI, use of SI for staff and faculty development, benefits of SI for both the students and the SI leaders, statistical research reports, and eight case studies illustrating the experience of implementing SI in British higher education courses.

Rye, P. D., & Wallace, J. (1994). Supplemental Instruction: A peer-group learning program for medical undergraduates. *Nordisk Medicin, 109*(11), 307.

This article describes the use of SI with Norwegian undergraduate medical students. Various benefits of SI are described for the session participants: study strategies, life-long learning skills, and working in learning teams with other students.

Stansbury, S. L. (2001). Accelerated learning groups enhance Supplemental Instruction for at-risk students. *Journal of Developmental Education, 24*(3), 20-22, 24, 26, 28, 40.

In order to increase SI attendance, Accelerated Learning Groups (ALGs) were developed. A pilot study investigated whether at-risk students who participated in an ALG/SI combination demonstrated higher self-efficacy and SI attendance than those who participated in only SI. Results suggested that at-risk students were more likely to participate in 12 or more SI sessions if they attended an ALG/SI combination than if they attended only SI. In addition, the range of final grades was higher for those who attended an ALG/SI combination than for those who attended only SI.

Stone, M. E., & Jacobs, G. (Eds.). (2006). *Supplemental Instruction: New visions for empowering student learning* (New Directions for Teaching and Learning, No. 106). San Francisco: Jossey-Bass.

This sourcebook includes chapters on learning strategies; the basic SI model; SI at community colleges; a credit-bearing training course for SI leaders; video-based SI; benefits to SI leaders and to faculty, administration, and institutions; and the future of SI.

Stone, M. E., Jacobs, G., & Hayes, H. (2006). Supplemental Instruction: Student perspectives in the 21st century. In D. B. Lundell, J. L. Higbee, I. M. Duranczyk, & E. Goff (Eds.), *Student standpoints about access programs in higher education* (pp. 129-141). Minneapolis, MN: Center for Research on Developmental Education and Urban Literacy, General College, University of Minnesota.

Using SI course survey results, this qualitative study examined students' and SI leaders' perceptions of the benefits and challenges of SI.

Taksa, I., & Goldberg, R. (2004). Web-delivered Supplemental Instruction: Dynamic customizing of search algorithms to enhance independent learning for developmental mathematics students. *Mathematics and Computer Education, 38*(2), 152-164.

SI was modified for web delivery to increase its use and effectiveness of results for students. The focus was on serving developmental math students at the City University of New York.

Visor, J. N., Johnson, J. J., & Cole, L. N. (1992). The relationship of Supplemental Instruction to affect. *Journal of Developmental Education, 16*(2), 12-14, 16-18.

This SI study that examined college students enrolled in an introductory psychology course conducted at Illinois State University (Normal, IL). The noncognitive factors examined were locus of control, self-efficacy, and self-esteem. Results suggested that those who participated regularly in SI were affectively different from those who participated only occasionally or not at all.

Wallace, J. (1996). Peer tutoring: A collaborative approach. In S. Wolfendale, & J. Corbett (Eds.), *Opening doors: Learning support in higher education* (pp. 101-116). London, England: Cassell Publishers.

This chapter is a description of how the SI program was customized for use in the United Kingdom. The key to the success of the program was raising awareness for academic staff, the training of the student leaders, and the effective management of the scheme. Quotations from SI leaders and faculty members cite a variety of reasons for support for the SI program.

Wilcox, F. K., & Koehler, C. (1996). Supplemental Instruction: Critical thinking and academic assistance. *Metropolitan Universities: An International Forum, 6*(4), 87-99.

This article provides a basic overview of the SI including data from the University of Missouri – Kansas City. The study reviewed data from a geographically and institutionally diverse group of 146 institutions that used SI in 2,875 courses of diverse academic areas with an enrollment of 298,629 students. The data suggest that SI participants earned higher mean final course grades; higher percent of A and B final course grades; and a lower rate of Ds, Fs, and course withdrawals.

Wolfe, R. F. (1990). Professional development through peer interaction. *The Journal of Professional Studies, 14*(1), 50-57.

The SI program at Anne Arundel Community College (Arnold, MD) was modified to use faculty members as SI supervisors. While this was the initial focus for the faculty members, the mentor role evolved into an opportunity for them to observe colleagues and to grow as teachers.

Wright, G. L., Wright, R. R., & Lamb, C. E. (2002). Developmental mathematics education and Supplemental Instruction: Pondering the potential. *Journal of Developmental Education, 26*(1), 30-35.

During the spring, summer, and fall 2000 semesters, data were gathered and analyzed concerning the effective use of SI in 90 developmental mathematics courses. The study monitored student outcomes in a small pilot program conducted at a southern state university with about 11,000 students. The student outcomes suggested that SI may have made a positive difference in the performance and retention rates of developmental mathematics students when the instructor was actively involved in promoting the SI group and certain modifications were made to the traditional role of the SI leader in the classroom.

Yockey, F. A., & George, A. A. (2000). The effects of a freshman seminar paired with Supplemental Instruction. *Journal of The First-Year Experience and Students in Transition, 10*(2), 57-76.

This study examines the impact on student performance of one section of a model first-year seminar, which is paired with an introductory-level core social science course. The seminar instructor attends the core course, takes notes and exams, does class projects, models good student behaviors, and leads a weekly review of the core course material, which is presented in a model similar to SI. The results indicate that students in the first-year seminar paired with SI achieved significantly higher grades in the paired core course, attained significantly higher semester grade point averages for the semester of intervention, and had significantly better retention rates after two years than students in the control group.

Zaritsky, J. S. (2001). Supplemental Instruction at an urban community college. In J. E. Miller, J. E. Groccia, & M. S. Miller (Eds.), *Student-assisted teaching: A guide to faculty-student teamwork* (pp. 103-108). Bolton, MA: Anker Publishing Company.

SI is used at LaGuardia Community College in New York to serve an ethnically diverse student body. After providing a general overview of the SI model, a 1997-98 research study is shared that analyzed the impact of the program with courses in accounting, computer science, biology, and chemistry. Overall mean final course grades favored the SI participants who earned a higher percentage of successful grades than nonparticipants.

About the
Contributors

Study Session 7 p.m.

David Arendale is an assistant professor in the Department of Postsecondary Teaching and Learning, College of Education and Human Development, University of Minnesota-Twin Cities.

Jennifer Carnicom is associate campus SI coordinator for the University of Missouri – Kansas City's Center for Academic Development. She received a master's degree in special education with an emphasis on learning disabilities in 2003 from the University of Missouri – Kansas City. Jennifer has also served as a video-based Supplemental Instruction facilitator for Western Civilization to 1600 courses for both high school and college students.

Melinda Gilbert earned a master's degree of counseling and guidance and served as graduate intern at the Center for Academic Development and the International Center for SI at the University of Missouri – Kansas City.

Maureen Hurley has worked at the International Center for SI at the University of Missouri – Kansas City (UMKC) for 15 years and currently serves as an associate director. As a certified trainer, she has conducted a number of SI training workshops at colleges and universities and has also made presentations on SI at various conferences, both nationally and internationally. She received her interdisciplinary PhD in urban leadership and policy studies in education at UMKC in 2000.

Glen Jacobs is the director of the Center for Academic Development and the International Center for SI. He began his academic career in South Africa and did his doctoral research through a Fulbright Scholarship under the guidance of Deanna Martin, the founder of SI, at the University of Missouri – Kansas City (UMKC). He completed his doctoral degree at the University of Port Elizabeth – South Africa. Before coming to UMKC, he was chairman and director of the Department of Educational Services and professor of medical education at St. George's University School of Medicine. A national and international educator, Jacobs has done more than 60 conference presentations and workshops throughout Europe, the United States, South Africa, Australia, Canada, Mexico, and the Caribbean. Recently, the Center received a Missouri Senate Resolution in Honor of Supplemental Instruction.

Amelia McDaniel is a certified trainer of SI who has worked with the International Center for SI for six years. She began as an SI leader and part-time data assistant, helped supervise leaders as an SI mentor, and became a full-time assistant coordinator of the University of Missouri – Kansas City (UMKC) campus SI program in June 2002. Her academic degrees include a B.A. in philosophy and an M.A. in English literature, both from UMKC.

Sonny Painter has worked with the International Center for SI for six years. With a background in math education and computer science, Sonny began his journey with Supplemental Instruction as an SI leader and worked his way up the ranks as an SI Mentor, VSI facilitator, and is currently the assistant VSI coordinator. His involvement in SI has afforded him opportunities to present nationally and internationally, train higher education personnel internationally, and now publish on the subject. Currently, Sonny is working on his PhD in distance education and continues to research online learning environments. He also grasps any opportunity to teach on the subjects of math and technology integration.

Kay Lutjen Patterson was involved with video-based Supplemental Instruction (VSI) for 15 years and was instrumental in the development and evolution of VSI courses. She worked with faculty and deans to promote and produce VSI courses. She promoted VSI in rural Missouri high schools and developed trainings for the high school facilitators and orientation for the principals and superintendents. Internationally, she helped launch VSI in South Africa and the Northwest Territory of Canada. She received one of two outstanding presentation awards at the 2000 Retain Conference at the University of Northern British Columbia. She is a certified SI trainer, having helped with more than 20 institutions bring SI to their campuses.

Marion E. Stone, PhD, is associate director/research coordinator of the Center for Academic Development and the International Center for SI at the University of Missouri – Kansas City. She is a certified SI trainer. Her degrees include a B.A. in psychology and an M.S. and PhD in counseling psychology, all from the University of Kansas.

M. Lisa Stout, PhD, is the coordinator for the Math and Science Resource Center and special projects for the Center for Academic Development and the International Center for SI at the University of Missouri – Kansas City. She is a certified SI trainer. Her degrees include a B.A. in psychology/sociology from Drury University in Springfield, Missouri, and a master's and doctorate in counseling psychology from the University of Missouri, Columbia.

F. Kim Wilcox, PhD, has been the national coordinator of training for Supplemental Instruction at the University of Missouri – Kansas City for the last 15 years. He has trained more than 1,000 colleges and universities in Supplemental Instruction, presented or given keynote addresses at more than 75 educational conferences and published articles and chapters about issues related to student academic assistance programs. Wilcox has served as a university and corporate consultant at more than 50 colleges and businesses. He is also a member of the faculty in the Department of Speech and Drama at Metropolitan Community College-Penn Valley.

Sandra Zerger's undergraduate and master's degrees are in English, with a special emphasis on the study of language. For her PhD in curriculum and instruction, she emphasized faculty evaluation, both in the quantitative and naturalistic inquiry procedures. Her dissertation and area of specialty is in discipline-specific higher literacy. For 20 years, she was a faculty member in English and held various administrative positions, such as dean of freshmen, at Bethel College in North Newton, KS. She has also been a certified trainer for Supplemental Instruction since 1981. She is the former campus Supplemental Instruction coordinator at the International Center for SI at the University of Missouri – Kansas City. She developed curriculum for Supplemental Instruction, including the *Supplemental Instruction Leader Resource Manual* and the *Supplemental Instruction Mentor Manual*. She has conducted faculty development workshops and supervisor trainings nationally and internationally.